"There is only one corner of the universe you can be certain of improving, and that's your own self."

– Aldous Huxley

Copyright © 2025 by Maxx Weston

All rights reserved. No part of this publication may be reproduced, distributed, or transmitted in any form or by any means, including photocopying, recording, or other electronic or mechanical methods, without the prior written permission of the publisher, except in the case of brief quotations embodied in critical reviews and specific other noncommercial uses permitted by copyright law.

For permission requests, please contact the publisher at:

Books to Hook Publishing, LLC.

This book is a work of nonfiction. While every effort has been made to ensure accuracy, the author and publisher assume no responsibility for errors or omissions. The information provided is for educational and informational purposes and is not a substitute for professional advice. Readers should consult a qualified professional before deciding on mental health, wellness, or other areas covered in this book.

ISBN: 979-8-89283-225-0

First Edition: 2025

Cover design by Muqaddas

Printed in the United States of America

Table Of Contents

Introduction   **3**

Chapter 1: The Gen X Mindset: Breaking Free from Overload   **6**

    Section 1: The Unique Struggles of Gen X   6

    Section 2: Understanding Mental Overload   11

    Section 3: Shifting the Mindset   16

Chapter 2: Building the Foundation: Mental and Physical Wellness   **21**

    Section 1: The Mind-Body Connection   21

    Section 2: Identifying Triggers   26

    Section 3: Building a Wellness Routine   31

Chapter 3: Mastering Stress in a Chaotic World   **36**

    Section 1: Understanding Stress   36

    Section 2: Techniques to Manage Stress   41

    Section 3: Creating Your Stress Toolbox   46

Chapter 4: Emotional Fitness: Mastering Your Inner World — 52

Section 1: Understanding Your Emotions — 52

Section 2: Tools to Regulate Emotions — 57

Section 3: Building Emotional Resilience — 62

Chapter 5: Reconnecting with Your Purpose — 67

Section 1: Finding Clarity in Midlife — 67

Section 2: Discovering Your "Why" — 71

Section 3: Living with Intention — 76

Chapter 6: Strengthening Connections: Relationships That Uplift — 81

Section 1: The Power of Social Connection — 81

Section 2: Building Better Relationships — 86

Section 3: Strengthening Your Inner Circle — 90

Chapter 7: Thriving in a Digital World — 95

Section 1: Understanding Digital Overload — 95

Section 2: Taking Control of Technology — 100

Section 3: Using Technology to Thrive — 104

Chapter 8: The Mental Fitness Blueprint for Life   110

Section 1: Maintaining Momentum   110

Section 2: Sustaining Mental Fitness Long-Term   115

Section 3: Thriving Beyond the Noise   121

Acknowledgments

Writing this book has been an incredible journey that would not have been possible without the support, encouragement, and love of so many people. It takes more than just one person to bring a book to life, and I am deeply grateful for "my village" to have walked this path with me.

First and foremost, all glory be to God. Through HIM all things are possible.

To my mother, Judi—your love, wisdom, and guidance have shaped me into who I am today. Your strength and resilience have always been a beacon of light for me, and I carry those lessons daily. Thank you for instilling in me the values of perseverance, kindness, and the importance of following my passion.

Your insights have been invaluable to my family, friends, mentors, therapists, and colleagues, who have offered wisdom, encouragement, and feedback. Every conversation, piece of advice, and word of support has contributed to the pages of this book. I am grateful for your time and generosity.

And most importantly, thank you to you, the reader. Thank you for reading this book, investing in your mental fitness, and being open to growth and transformation. You are here, engaging with these ideas, so you are committed to building a better, healthier, and more resilient version of yourself. That is no small thing. I hope the words in these pages are a source of encouragement, clarity, and empowerment on your journey.

Thank you for being a part of this journey with me. If you found this book's information valuable/helpful, please take a few minutes to leave a review for your friends and neighbors to view.

This book will lead to a more balanced, fulfilling, and thriving life.

Introduction

Why This Book Matters

Generation X stands at a unique crossroads. Born between the early 1960s and late 1970s, Gen Xers grew up in a world before the digital revolution but have since had to adapt to its rapid expansion. They are often called the "sandwich generation," balancing careers, raising children, and caring for aging parents while navigating financial pressures, shifting societal expectations, and a fast-paced digital landscape.

For many Gen Xers, life has been about endurance—pushing through, taking responsibility, and handling problems independently. But decades of "just getting by" can take a toll. The constant juggling act often leaves little room for self-care, reflection, or genuine well-being. It's no wonder that stress, anxiety, and burnout are at all-time highs for this generation.

Yet, amid these challenges, there is an opportunity. Rather than remaining in survival mode, Gen Xers can redefine what mental fitness means. This book is about shifting from just getting through the day to actively thriving. It's about developing resilience, emotional intelligence, and sustainable habits that foster balance and fulfillment.

Mental fitness is no longer just about avoiding burnout—it's about proactively cultivating a life that aligns with your values, priorities, and aspirations. This book is designed to help you do just that.

What You'll Gain

This isn't another self-help book filled with vague advice and generic platitudes. *Thriving Through the Noise: Gen X's Mental Health Playbook* is a practical guide tailored to the real-life struggles and responsibilities of Gen Xers. Inside, you'll find:

- A practical playbook for managing stress, emotions, and mindset. You'll learn how to handle daily challenges more efficiently and build habits that support long-term well-being.

- Tools to build resilience and create balance. Rather than feeling pulled in several directions, you'll develop strategies to prioritize what matters most and let go of what doesn't serve you.

- Actionable strategies for long-term mental fitness. Small, consistent actions lead to lasting change. This book provides step-by-step methods to help you incorporate mental fitness into your daily life, no matter how busy.

The goal isn't perfection—it's progress. Applying these strategies will build a foundation for mental clarity, emotional strength, and a renewed sense of purpose.

How to Use This Book

This book is designed to be approachable, practical, and easy to implement, even amid a hectic schedule. You don't need to read it all at once; you can work through it at your own pace, applying concepts as they fit into your life. Here's how the book is structured:

1. **Understanding Mental Fitness** – The first few chapters provide a new framework for mental health, emphasizing the mind-body connection, stress management, and emotional awareness.

2. **Mastering Stress and Emotions** – Learn how to handle life's challenges more resiliently, regulate emotions effectively, and break free from negative thought patterns.

3. **Building Stronger Connections** – Relationships play a huge role in mental well-being. This section helps you navigate friendships, family dynamics, and setting boundaries.

4. **Thriving in a Digital World** – Technology is both a tool and a distraction. You'll learn how to use it intentionally to support, rather than sabotage, your mental fitness.

5. **Living with Purpose and Balance** – The final chapters help you reconnect with what truly matters, prioritize joy, and develop a long-term mental fitness routine that fits your life.

Each chapter includes actionable steps, real-life examples, and reflection exercises to help you put theory into practice. The goal is to integrate small, manageable changes into your daily routine—adjustments that create a big impact over time.

By the end of this book, you'll have a personalized mental fitness plan that aligns with your lifestyle, values, and responsibilities. More importantly, you'll have the confidence and tools to navigate life's ups and downs with resilience, clarity, and purpose.

Final Thoughts: A New Approach to Mental Well-Being

Mental fitness isn't about fixing what's broken but strengthening what's already within you. You don't need to overhaul your entire life to see results. Small, intentional changes, repeated consistently, will help you shift from simply surviving to truly thriving.

Thriving Through the Noise is your playbook if you're ready to take charge of your mental health, build resilience, and create a balanced and fulfilling life. Let's get started.

Chapter 1: The Gen X Mindset: Breaking Free from Overload

"Do what you can, with what you have, where you are." – Theodore Roosevelt

Section 1: The Unique Struggles of Gen X

As members of Generation X, born between the mid-1960s and early 1980s, you've grown accustomed to carrying the weight of responsibility. Labeled the "latchkey kids," you learned independence early, often coming home to empty houses and navigating the world alone while your parents worked. Over time, that self-reliance turned into resilience and planted the seeds of chronic stress. Today, Gen X faces a unique set of challenges that exacerbate this stress—challenges that can leave even the most capable feeling stretched to their limits.

From managing the dual demands of aging parents and adult children to navigating midlife career transitions and keeping pace with the constant demands of technology, you are, in many ways, caught in the middle of competing forces. These struggles are often overwhelming, yet they remain largely unacknowledged. Let's dive deeper into three defining stressors that uniquely impact Gen X: caregiving as the "sandwich generation," career burnout, and digital overload.

The Sandwich Generation: Caring for Aging Parents and Supporting Adult Kids Simultaneously

One of the most defining features of life as a Gen Xer is the dual caregiving role you often occupy. Dubbed the "sandwich generation," you're wedged between two significant responsibilities: caring for aging parents while still supporting your children, many of whom are entering adulthood but remain financially or emotionally dependent.

This dual role comes with immense pressure. On one side, your parents may require increasing levels of care as they age, from managing medical appointments and financial decisions to providing emotional support. Conversely, your children may still be navigating major life transitions, such as completing their education, starting careers, or forming their own families. The result? You're being pulled in opposite directions with little time or energy left for yourself.

The Emotional Toll of Caregiving

Caring for aging parents often brings a mix of emotions—gratitude for the opportunity to give back, guilt for not being able to do enough, and sadness as you witness their decline. You may feel obligated to take on the lion's share of responsibility, even as it impacts your mental and physical health.

On the other hand, supporting adult children has its challenges. Whether it's helping them pay off student loans, providing a place to live, or offering emotional guidance as they navigate an increasingly uncertain world, you may feel torn between wanting to help and encouraging their independence.

The Financial Strain

Beyond the emotional toll, the financial strain of being the "sandwich generation" is significant. Many Gen Xers are dipping into retirement savings to cover their children's education or supplement their parents' medical expenses. This creates a precarious financial situation, leaving little room for personal goals or future planning.

Balancing the Load

While the demands of caregiving are undeniable, there are strategies to reduce the burden. Sharing responsibilities with siblings or other family members, seeking professional support like eldercare services, and encouraging your children to take on more responsibilities are all ways to create balance. Most importantly, learning to set boundaries and prioritize your needs is critical. It's impossible to pour from an empty cup, and your mental health must be a priority if you're to sustain the caregiving role.

Navigating Career Pressure: Burnout and Managing Midlife Career Transitions

In addition to caregiving, Gen X faces unique challenges in the workplace. You're in the prime of your career, yet many of you feel stuck in the middle—caught between younger colleagues climbing the corporate ladder and older colleagues holding on to leadership roles. You may feel overlooked, undervalued, or irrelevant in an increasingly digital and youth-oriented workplace culture.

The Reality of Burnout

Burnout has become a pervasive issue for Gen X. You've spent decades working hard, often in environments that demand more with fewer resources. The pressure to perform at a high level while balancing personal responsibilities can lead to chronic stress, fatigue, and disengagement. This is particularly true for those in high-stress professions or those who are self-employed and carry the added responsibility of running a business.

For many, the pandemic exacerbated these feelings of burnout. The shift to remote work blurred the professional and personal life boundaries, creating an "always-on" culture that makes it difficult to unplug.

Midlife Career Transitions

Adding to the pressure is the reality of midlife career transitions. You may question whether your current career aligns with your values or long-term goals. Some Gen Xers are considering pivots to new industries, while others are grappling with job insecurity in fields that are evolving rapidly due to automation and technological advancements. These transitions can feel daunting, especially when combined with financial responsibilities and the fear of starting over.

Reclaiming Career Satisfaction

The good news is that midlife is an ideal time to reassess your career and make changes that align with your priorities. Whether negotiating a better work-life balance, pursuing a passion project, or developing new skills, there are opportunities to redefine your professional life. Setting boundaries around work is also crucial, such as limiting after-hours communication and taking regular breaks to recharge.

The Rise of Digital Overload: Social Media, Constant News, and Technology Stress

Another defining stressor for Gen X is the rise of digital overload. As the first generation to straddle both analog and digital worlds, you've witnessed the transformation of technology from a tool to a constant companion. While technology has brought incredible convenience, it's also introduced new forms of stress that impact your mental health.

The Social Media Trap

Social media, in particular, has become a double-edged sword. On one hand, it's a valuable way to stay connected with friends, family, and colleagues. On the other hand, it can lead to feelings of inadequacy, comparison, and even anxiety. The curated highlight reels of others' lives often create unrealistic expectations and amplify the fear of missing out (FOMO).

For Gen X, who grew up without social media, this constant exposure to other people's lives can feel overwhelming. You may find yourself scrolling mindlessly through feeds, only to feel worse afterward.

The Pressure of Constant News

In addition to social media, the 24/7 news cycle contributes to digital overload. With breaking news notifications and endless headlines, it's easy to feel bombarded by negative information. This constant influx of news can fuel anxiety, especially during global uncertainty or crisis.

The Impact on Mental Health

The cumulative effect of digital overload is significant. Studies show excessive screen time can lead to increased stress, disrupted sleep, and diminished focus. It can also create a disconnection, even as we're more "connected" than ever.

Taking Back Control

Managing digital overload requires intentionality. Simple strategies like setting limits on social media usage, turning off push notifications, and designating tech-free zones in your home can help you reclaim your time and mental space. Incorporating mindfulness practices, such as taking breaks to unplug or spending time in nature, can also counteract the adverse effects of digital stress.

Conclusion

The unique struggles of Gen X are undeniable. As the "sandwich generation," you're balancing caregiving responsibilities that pull you in opposite directions. In the workplace, you're grappling with burnout and navigating midlife career transitions. And in an increasingly digital world, you face social media challenges, constant news, and technology stress.

These pressures may feel overwhelming, but they don't have to define you. You can break free from the overload cycle by acknowledging these challenges and taking intentional steps to address them. The following chapters will provide the tools and strategies to empower you to move from survival mode to a place where you can thrive.

Section 2: Understanding Mental Overload

Mental overload is an all-too-familiar experience for Generation X. The relentless juggling of responsibilities and the fast pace of modern life can leave you feeling overwhelmed and perpetually drained. But to break free from the cycle of mental overload, you first need to understand it—what it does to your brain and body, how to identify the stressors unique to your life, and, most importantly, how to stop the mental "hamster wheel" that keeps you spinning in place.

The Science of Overwhelm: How Constant Stress Impacts Brain and Body

Stress is a natural and necessary part of life. It helps you stay alert, motivated, and ready to respond to challenges. But when stress becomes chronic—when it feels like there's no off switch—it starts to wreak havoc on your brain and body. This state of constant overwhelm is not sustainable, and its effects can manifest in ways that undermine your physical health, emotional stability, and overall well-being.

What Happens in Your Brain

When faced with a stressor, your brain activates the fight-or-flight response, a survival mechanism designed to protect you from immediate danger. This response is triggered by the amygdala, the part of the brain responsible for processing emotions and detecting threats. The amygdala signals the hypothalamus, releasing stress hormones like cortisol and adrenaline.

In short bursts, this response is helpful—it heightens your senses, sharpens your focus, and prepares your body for action. But when stress is constant, the brain remains in this heightened state for too long. The result? Your prefrontal cortex, the part of the brain responsible for decision-making, problem-solving, and self-control, starts to go offline. Chronic stress makes thinking, regulating emotions, and responding rationally to situations harder.

Over time, prolonged exposure to stress hormones can shrink the hippocampus, the part of the brain involved in memory and learning. This is why mental overload often feels like a fog—you can't concentrate, remember important details, or make decisions effectively.

The Toll on Your Body

The physical effects of chronic stress are just as damaging. Elevated cortisol levels can lead to:

- **Weakened immune function**, making you more susceptible to illness.
- **Increased inflammation** is linked to conditions like heart disease, diabetes, and autoimmune disorders.
- **Digestive problems**, as stress disrupts the gut-brain connection.
- **Sleep disturbances** lead to a vicious cycle where poor rest exacerbates stress.

This constant state of hypervigilance also drains your energy reserves, leaving you feeling physically exhausted even when you've done little physical activity.

Why Gen X Is Especially Prone to Overwhelm

As a Gen Xer, you've likely spent decades in low-grade stress, balancing work, family, and societal expectations. The cumulative effect of these pressures means your stress response system may be stuck in overdrive. And because you've been conditioned to "power through," you might not even realize the toll it's taking until it becomes unmanageable.

Identifying Triggers: Recognizing Stressors Unique to Your Life

One of the most effective ways to reduce mental overload is to identify and address your specific stress triggers. While some stressors are universal, others are deeply personal, shaped by your unique circumstances and experiences.

Everyday Stress Triggers for Gen X

- **Workplace Demands** : Whether you're climbing the career ladder, managing a midlife career shift, or trying to stay relevant in a rapidly changing workforce, career pressures constitute a significant source of stress.

- **Family Responsibilities** : The dual demands of caring for aging parents and supporting children can create constant tension. You may feel pulled in opposite directions, with little time for yourself.

- **Financial Pressures** : Financial stress is a constant for many Gen Xers, from paying off mortgages to saving for retirement and helping children with college expenses.

- **Technology Overload** : The endless stream of emails, notifications, and social media updates can leave you feeling tethered to your devices and unable to disconnect.

The Importance of Self-Awareness

Not all triggers are external; some are internal, rooted in your thoughts, beliefs, and habits. For example:

- **Perfectionism** : The belief that you must excel at everything can create unnecessary pressure.

- **People-Pleasing** : Saying yes to every request, even at the expense of your well-being, can lead to overwhelm.

- **Negative Self-Talk** : Constantly criticizing yourself or doubting your abilities can amplify stress.

Start by paying attention to your emotional and physical responses to identify your triggers. Do certain situations leave you feeling anxious, irritable, or drained? Do you notice tension in your shoulders, headaches, or an upset stomach? These are clues that point to the sources of your stress.

Practical Steps to Manage Triggers

Once you've identified your stressors, you can take steps to address them:

1. **Set Boundaries** : Learn to say no to commitments that don't align with your priorities.
2. **Delegate Responsibilities** : Share the load, whether at work or home.
3. **Challenge Negative Beliefs** : Replace unhelpful thoughts with affirming ones, such as "I'm doing the best I can."

Breaking the Cycle: How to Stop the Mental "Hamster Wheel"

One of the most frustrating aspects of mental overload is the sense that your mind is constantly racing. Thoughts loop endlessly, replaying worries or imagining worst-case scenarios. This mental "hamster wheel" drains your energy and prevents you from taking meaningful action.

Why the Hamster Wheel Happens

A combination of often fuels the mental hamster wheel:

- **Unresolved Stress** : When you don't address stressors directly, they linger in your mind, creating a sense of unfinished business.
- **Perfectionism** : The fear of making mistakes or falling short can keep your mind stuck in overthinking mode.
- **Lack of Mindfulness** : Staying grounded in the present is

problematic when you're constantly focused on the future or ruminating on the past.

Strategies to Break Free

Practice Mindfulness

Mindfulness is the art of bringing one's attention to the present moment without judgment. It helps one break the cycle of rumination by shifting one's focus away from unproductive thoughts.

- Start with simple practices, like focusing on your breath for a few minutes daily.
- Use mindfulness apps or guided meditations to build consistency.

Take Action

Often, the hamster wheel spins because you're stuck in indecision. Even small steps to address a problem can create momentum and reduce mental clutter.

- Break tasks into manageable pieces.
- Focus on what you can control rather than what's outside your influence.

Schedule Worry Time

This may sound counterintuitive, but scheduling a specific time to worry can help you relieve stress. For example, set aside 15 minutes in the evening to jot down your concerns and brainstorm solutions. Knowing you have dedicated time to address worries can prevent them from dominating your day.

Engage in Physical Activity

Exercise is one of the most effective ways to disrupt the mental hamster wheel. Physical activity reduces cortisol levels, releases endorphins, and helps clear your mind. Even a 10-minute walk can make a difference.

Limit Information Overload

Too much information—news, social media, or emails—can feed the hamster wheel. Set boundaries around your media consumption, such as turning off notifications or limiting screen time in the evenings.

Conclusion

Understanding mental overload is the first step to overcoming it. By learning how chronic stress impacts your brain and body, identifying your unique triggers, and implementing strategies to break the mental hamster wheel, you can regain control of your mind and create a calmer, more balanced life.

The pressures of being a Gen Xer are real, but they don't have to define your experience. In the next section, we'll explore practical tools and techniques to build mental fitness and start thriving, even in the face of life's challenges. Remember, breaking free from overload isn't about doing everything perfectly—it's about taking intentional steps to care for yourself and create a life of clarity, resilience, and purpose.

Section 3: Shifting the Mindset

The Gen X generation, often characterized as resourceful, resilient, and self-reliant, has weathered immense societal and personal shifts. From growing up as latchkey kids to becoming the backbone of workplaces and families, this generation knows all too well the weight of responsibility. Yet, with the increasing pace of life, the digital deluge, and the demands of balancing multiple roles, it's easy to fall into overload patterns. Shifting this mindset isn't about doing more or striving harder—it's about consciously transforming how we think, act, and prioritize.

The Power of Awareness: How Self-Awareness Sets the Stage for Change

Awareness is the cornerstone of any significant transformation. Before addressing the overwhelming pressure that dominates our lives, we must first recognize its existence and the subtle ways it creeps in. For Gen Xers, this means taking a step back from the busyness of life to assess the patterns driving daily decisions.

Self-awareness begins with asking powerful questions:

- What are the sources of stress in my life?
- How do I react to challenges, and are those reactions serving me well?
- Am I prioritizing what truly matters, or am I running on autopilot?

Many Gen Xers are conditioned to push through challenges, believing resilience means bearing more without breaking. However, true resilience comes from knowing when to pause and recalibrate. Self-awareness allows us to identify the underlying beliefs that keep us stuck in cycles of overcommitment, such as the idea that "success equals busyness" or "I must do it all to be valuable."

Awareness also creates space for mindfulness, a practice that anchors us in the present moment rather than the constant churn of worries about the past or future. Mental clarity can be the difference between feeling overwhelmed and feeling empowered. Simple practices like journaling, meditating, or setting aside moments for reflection can cultivate a deeper understanding of our thoughts and emotions.

When Gen Xers embrace self-awareness, they unlock the ability to challenge long-held beliefs and habits that no longer serve them. Awareness is not about judgment but curiosity. It's about observing oneself compassionately and asking, "How can I create a life aligned with my values and needs?"

Letting Go of Perfectionism: Embracing Imperfection as a Strength

Perfectionism is a double-edged sword. While striving for excellence can lead to impressive accomplishments, it can create immense pressure and unrealistic expectations. For Gen Xers, pursuing perfection often stems from societal norms or early experiences of having to prove their worth. This drive for flawlessness can seep into every aspect of life—careers, parenting, relationships, and even self-care—leaving little room for rest or imperfection.

Letting go of perfectionism requires a mindset shift: recognizing that imperfection is not a failure but a natural and necessary part of being human. Brené Brown, a prominent researcher on vulnerability and shame, emphasizes that imperfection is the birthplace of creativity, connection, and authenticity. By accepting imperfections, Gen Xers can free themselves from the endless pursuit of unattainable standards and instead focus on what truly matters.

One strategy for releasing perfectionism is to reframe mistakes as opportunities for growth. For example, rather than viewing a missed deadline or a parenting misstep as a personal failure, it can be seen as a chance to learn and adapt. This mindset not only reduces stress but also fosters resilience.

Another powerful approach is to embrace vulnerability. Perfectionism often masks a fear of judgment or rejection, but when we allow ourselves to be seen as we are—flaws and all—we cultivate more profound, meaningful connections. This openness also encourages others to let go of their perfectionistic tendencies, creating a ripple effect of authenticity.

Finally, Gen Xers can practice self-compassion. Instead of holding themselves to impossible standards, they can treat themselves with the kindness and understanding they would offer a close friend. Self-compassion acknowledges that everyone struggles, and it's okay to stumble on the path to progress.

By letting go of perfectionism, Gen Xers reduce their mental and emotional load and open the door to a more fulfilling, balanced life. Imperfection is not a weakness—it's a strength that reminds us to focus on what truly matters: growth, connection, and joy.

Choosing to Thrive: Reclaiming Control Over Your Mental Space

Thriving is a choice. It's not a passive state of being but an active decision to prioritize well-being and joy despite life's challenges. For Gen Xers, reclaiming control over their mental space starts with recognizing their agency—the ability to make choices that align with their values and aspirations.

One of the first steps to choosing to thrive is setting boundaries. Gen Xers often juggle work, family, and community demands, leaving little room for personal needs. Learning to say "no" to unnecessary obligations and "yes" to self-care is a powerful act of reclaiming control. Boundaries create the mental and emotional space needed to focus on what truly matters.

Another essential aspect of thriving is redefining success. Many Gen Xers grew up with traditional markers of achievement—financial stability, career advancement, and material possessions. While these are valid goals, they often come at the expense of inner peace and happiness. Thriving means expanding the definition of success to include well-being, meaningful relationships, and personal fulfillment.

Mindfulness and gratitude practices can also significantly contribute to fostering a thriving mindset. By focusing on the present moment and appreciating the positive aspects of life, Gen Xers can shift their perspective from scarcity to abundance. Even small rituals, like pausing to savor a cup of coffee or reflecting on three things you're grateful for daily, can transform mental habits and promote a sense of contentment.

Thriving also requires a commitment to self-care. This doesn't just mean spa days or vacations—it's about consistently nurturing physical, mental, and emotional health. Exercise, healthy eating, adequate sleep, and moments of joy are non-negotiable for a thriving mindset.

Lastly, community and connection are vital. Thriving isn't a solo journey—it's about surrounding oneself with supportive people who uplift and inspire. Building connections fosters a sense of belonging and shared purpose, whether it's close friends, family, or a professional network.

Choosing to thrive is about reclaiming agency in a world that often feels out of control. It's about consciously prioritizing what matters most and letting go of the rest. For Gen Xers, this shift can lead to a life that is not just manageable but truly meaningful.

The Path Forward

Shifting the mindset from overload to empowerment is not an overnight transformation—it's a journey that requires patience, practice, and persistence. By embracing self-awareness, letting go of perfectionism, and choosing to thrive, Gen Xers can break free from the cycles of stress and busyness that have long defined their lives.

This shift is about more than just surviving the chaos—it's about reclaiming control, rediscovering joy, and creating a life that aligns with one's deepest values. The Gen X mindset is one of resilience and resourcefulness, and by consciously shifting perspectives, this generation has the power to lead by example, inspiring others to do the same.

The time for change is now. The question is not whether it's possible—but whether you're ready to take the first step toward a new way of thinking and living.

Chapter 2: Building the Foundation: Mental and Physical Wellness

"What lies behind us and what lies before us are tiny matters compared to what lies within us." – Ralph Waldo Emerson

Section 1: The Mind-Body Connection

The intricate relationship between the mind and body forms the cornerstone of holistic wellness. Understanding this dynamic interplay empowers individuals to foster mental resilience and illuminates how physical health profoundly impacts mental fitness. By delving into the critical elements of sleep, nutrition, movement, stress hormones, and energy management, we uncover actionable strategies to cultivate balance and vitality.

How Physical Health Impacts Mental Fitness Sleep: The Silent Pillar of Mental Wellness

Sleep is not just a period of rest; it's a critical process where the mind and body engage in essential maintenance. Adequate sleep supports cognitive functions like memory consolidation, problem-solving, and emotional regulation. On the flip side, chronic sleep deprivation can lead to mood disorders such as anxiety and depression.

During deep sleep, the brain clears out toxins and strengthens neural connections. REM sleep, the dream phase, plays a pivotal role in processing emotions and fostering creativity. However, poor sleep hygiene — irregular schedules, excessive screen time before bed, or consuming stimulants — disrupts these processes, impairing mental fitness.

To optimize sleep:

- **Prioritize Consistency**: Go to bed and wake up at the same time daily.
- **Create a Sleep-Conducive Environment**: Ensure a dark, quiet, and cool bedroom.
- **Practice Relaxation Techniques**: Deep breathing or meditation can calm the mind before sleep.

Nutrition: Fueling the Brain

Our food directly affects brain function, mood, and energy levels. A diet rich in whole foods — such as vegetables, fruits, lean proteins, and healthy fats — provides the nutrients necessary for optimal brain health. Key nutrients like omega-3 fatty acids, antioxidants, and B vitamins benefit mental clarity and emotional stability.

Conversely, diets high in processed foods, refined sugars, and unhealthy fats are linked to increased rates of depression and cognitive decline. Blood sugar fluctuations caused by these foods can lead to mood swings and fatigue, further compromising mental resilience.

Actionable tips for better nutrition:

- **Incorporate Brain-Boosting Foods**: Add fatty fish, nuts, seeds, and dark leafy greens to your diet.
- **Stay Hydrated**: Dehydration, even mild, can impair focus and memory.
- **Practice Mindful Eating**: Savor your meals without distractions to improve digestion and satisfaction.

Movement: Energizing the Mind

Regular physical activity is a powerful tool for mental health. Exercise boosts the production of endorphins, often called "happy hormones," which improve mood and reduce stress. It also enhances brain plasticity, aiding in learning and memory.

Activities like yoga and tai chi combine movement with mindfulness, reducing cortisol levels while increasing mental clarity. Even moderate activities such as walking or gardening can improve mood and alleviate symptoms of depression.

To harness the mental benefits of movement:

- **Find Activities You Enjoy**: Exercise shouldn't feel like a chore; choose activities that excite you.
- **Incorporate Movement Daily**: Aim for at least 30 minutes of moderate exercise most days.
- **Mix It Up**: Alternate between cardio, strength training, and flexibility exercises for holistic benefits.

Stress Hormones and Balance: Understanding Cortisol and Its Effects

Stress is unavoidable, but the body's response to stress can significantly impact mental and physical health. Central to this response is cortisol, a hormone released by the adrenal glands during stress.

The Role of Cortisol

Cortisol is essential for survival, helping the body respond to immediate threats by increasing energy availability and sharpening focus. However, chronic stress leads to prolonged cortisol elevation, which can:

- Impair memory and concentration.
- Suppress the immune system, making the body more vulnerable to illness. • Disrupt sleep, leading to a vicious cycle of fatigue and heightened stress.

Achieving Hormonal Balance

Managing cortisol levels involves cultivating habits that help the body recover from stress. Key strategies include:

- **Mindfulness Practices**: Meditation, deep breathing, and progressive muscle relaxation reduce stress and lower cortisol.
- **Social Connection**: Building and maintaining supportive relationships can buffer the effects of stress.
- **Adequate Rest**: Sleep and periods of intentional relaxation allow the body to reset.

The Impact of Unchecked Stress

When cortisol levels remain elevated over time, it can lead to burnout, characterized by emotional exhaustion, cynicism, and reduced productivity. Recognizing early signs of stress overload — irritability, brain fog, or frequent illnesses — is crucial to taking corrective action.

Energy as a Resource: Protecting and Replenishing Your Energy

Understanding Energy Dynamics

Energy is a finite resource, replenished through rest, nutrition, and self-care. Depleting this resource without replenishment leads to fatigue, diminished focus, and emotional imbalance. Viewing energy as a currency helps frame decisions around its conservation and restoration.

Strategies for Energy Management

1. **Protect Energy Through Boundaries:**
   - Say no to unnecessary commitments.
   - Limit exposure to energy-draining situations or people.

2. **Replenish Through Recovery:**
   - Engage in rejuvenating activities like hobbies, nature walks, or quiet reflection. ○ Prioritize "unplugged" time to disconnect from digital distractions.

3. **Balance Physical and Mental Exertion:**
   - Alternate between periods of intense focus and restorative breaks.
   - Use techniques like the Pomodoro method to maintain productivity without burnout.

The Role of Self-Awareness

Self-awareness is crucial in identifying energy drains and what activities or environments restore vitality. Journaling or tracking daily energy levels can uncover patterns and inform better decisions.

The Importance of Joy and Play

Joyful activities and moments of play are often overlooked but are essential for replenishing energy. Whether laughing with friends, engaging in a creative hobby, or playing a sport, these experiences restore mental and emotional balance.

Integrating Mind-Body Practices

Fostering the mind-body connection is a lifelong journey requiring intentionality and consistency. By prioritizing physical health through sleep, nutrition, and movement, managing stress hormones like cortisol, and protecting energy reserves, individuals can build a strong foundation for mental and physical wellness. The interplay between the mind and body underscores the importance of treating them as interconnected systems, where nurturing one invariably supports the other.

In this fast-paced world, small, deliberate actions compound into significant transformations. Honoring the mind-body connection unlocks the potential for resilience, balance, and thriving health.

Section 2: Identifying Triggers

The intricate relationship between the mind and body forms the cornerstone of holistic wellness. Understanding this dynamic interplay empowers individuals to foster mental resilience and illuminates how physical health profoundly impacts mental fitness. By delving into the critical elements of sleep, nutrition, movement, stress hormones, and energy management, we uncover actionable strategies to cultivate balance and vitality.

How Physical Health Impacts Mental Fitness

Sleep: The Silent Pillar of Mental Wellness

Sleep is not just a period of rest; it's a critical process where the mind and body engage in essential maintenance. Adequate sleep supports cognitive functions like memory consolidation, problem-solving, and emotional regulation. On the flip side, chronic sleep deprivation can lead to mood disorders such as anxiety and depression.

During deep sleep, the brain clears out toxins and strengthens neural connections. REM sleep, the dream phase, plays a pivotal role in processing emotions and fostering creativity. However, poor sleep hygiene — irregular schedules, excessive screen time before bed, or consuming stimulants — disrupts these processes, impairing mental fitness.

To optimize sleep:

- **Prioritize Consistency**: Go to bed and wake up at the same time daily.
- **Create a Sleep-Conducive Environment**: Ensure a dark, quiet, and cool bedroom.
- **Practice Relaxation Techniques**: Deep breathing or meditation can calm the mind before sleep.

Nutrition: Fueling the Brain

Our food directly affects brain function, mood, and energy levels. A diet rich in whole foods — such as vegetables, fruits, lean proteins, and healthy fats — provides the nutrients necessary for optimal brain health. Key nutrients like omega-3 fatty acids, antioxidants, and B vitamins are beneficial for mental clarity and emotional stability.

Conversely, diets high in processed foods, refined sugars, and unhealthy fats are linked to increased rates of depression and cognitive decline. Blood sugar fluctuations caused by these foods can lead to mood swings and fatigue, further compromising mental resilience.

Actionable tips for better nutrition:

- **Incorporate Brain-Boosting Foods**: Add fatty fish, nuts, seeds, and dark leafy greens to your diet.
- **Stay Hydrated**: Dehydration, even mild, can impair focus and memory.
- **Practice Mindful Eating**: Savor your meals without distractions to improve digestion and satisfaction.

Movement: Energizing the Mind

Regular physical activity is a powerful tool for mental health. Exercise boosts the production of endorphins, often called "happy hormones," which improve mood and reduce stress. It also enhances brain plasticity, aiding in learning and memory.

Activities like yoga and tai chi combine movement with mindfulness, reducing cortisol levels while increasing mental clarity. Even moderate activities such as walking or gardening can improve mood and alleviate symptoms of depression.

To harness the mental benefits of movement:

- **Find Activities You Enjoy**: Exercise shouldn't feel like a chore; choose activities that excite you.
- **Incorporate Movement Daily**: Aim for at least 30 minutes of moderate exercise most days.
- **Mix It Up**: Alternate between cardio, strength training, and flexibility exercises for holistic benefits.

Stress Hormones and Balance: Understanding Cortisol and Its Effects

Stress is unavoidable, but the body's response to stress can significantly impact mental and physical health. Central to this response is cortisol, a hormone released by the adrenal glands during stress.

The Role of Cortisol

Cortisol is essential for survival, helping the body respond to immediate threats by increasing energy availability and sharpening focus. However, chronic stress leads to prolonged cortisol elevation, which can:

- Impair memory and concentration.
- Suppress the immune system, making the body more vulnerable to illness.
- Disrupt sleep, leading to a vicious cycle of fatigue and heightened stress.

Achieving Hormonal Balance

Managing cortisol levels involves cultivating habits that help the body recover from stress. Key strategies include:

- **Mindfulness Practices**: Meditation, deep breathing, and progressive muscle relaxation reduce stress and lower cortisol.
- **Social Connection**: Building and maintaining supportive relationships can buffer the effects of stress.
- **Adequate Rest**: Sleep and periods of intentional relaxation

allow the body to reset.

The Impact of Unchecked Stress

When cortisol levels remain elevated over time, it can lead to burnout, characterized by emotional exhaustion, cynicism, and reduced productivity. Recognizing early signs of stress overload — irritability, brain fog, or frequent illnesses — is crucial to taking corrective action.

Energy as a Resource: Protecting and Replenishing Your Energy

Understanding Energy Dynamics

Energy is a finite resource, replenished through rest, nutrition, and self-care. Depleting this resource without replenishment leads to fatigue, diminished focus, and emotional imbalance. Viewing energy as a currency helps frame decisions around its conservation and restoration.

Strategies for Energy Management

1. **Protect Energy Through Boundaries**:
   - Say no to unnecessary commitments.
   - Limit exposure to energy-draining situations or people.

2. **Replenish Through Recovery**:
   - Engage in rejuvenating activities, such as hobbies, nature walks, or quiet reflection.
   - Prioritize "unplugged" time to disconnect from digital distractions.

3. **Balance Physical and Mental Exertion**:
   - Alternate between periods of intense focus and restorative breaks.
   - Use techniques like the Pomodoro method to maintain

productivity without burnout.

The Role of Self-Awareness

Self-awareness is crucial in identifying energy drains and what activities or environments restore vitality. Journaling or tracking daily energy levels can uncover patterns and inform better decisions.

The Importance of Joy and Play

Joyful activities and moments of play are often overlooked but are essential for replenishing energy. Whether laughing with friends, engaging in a creative hobby, or playing a sport, these experiences restore mental and emotional balance.

Integrating Mind-Body Practices

Fostering the mind-body connection is a lifelong journey requiring intentionality and consistency. By prioritizing physical health through sleep, nutrition, and movement, managing stress hormones like cortisol, and protecting energy reserves, individuals can build a strong foundation for mental and physical wellness. The interplay between the mind and body underscores the importance of treating them as interconnected systems, where nurturing one invariably supports the other.

In this fast-paced world, small, deliberate actions compound into significant transformations. Honoring the mind-body connection unlocks the potential for resilience, balance, and thriving health.

Section 3: Building a Wellness Routine

Creating a sustainable wellness routine is one of the most empowering steps toward achieving mental and physical well-being. However, developing this habit does not happen overnight. It requires small, intentional efforts, consistent tracking, and the resilience to overcome setbacks. Individuals can build a personalized routine that enhances their overall quality of life by focusing on these key elements.

Starting Small: Tiny Habits That Add Up

Many people make the mistake of aiming for drastic lifestyle changes, only to become overwhelmed and abandon their efforts. The key to a successful wellness routine is starting small and building upon simple, manageable habits that seamlessly integrate into daily life.

The Power of Tiny Habits

Small, repeatable actions compound over time to produce significant results. Research supports that tiny, sustainable habits are more effective than drastic, short-lived changes. Instead of aiming for an hour-long workout each day, one might begin with just five minutes of stretching or a short walk. Instead of attempting a complete dietary overhaul, adding one extra serving of vegetables per meal can create meaningful progress.

Some examples of small habits that contribute to wellness include:

- Drinking a glass of water first thing in the morning.
- Take five deep breaths before starting the day.
- Walking for ten minutes after meals.
- Journaling for two minutes before bed.
- Practicing gratitude by noting one positive thing daily.

Individuals are more likely to experience early successes by starting with small, achievable actions, reinforcing their motivation to continue. Over time, these habits naturally evolve, leading to more substantial changes without feeling overwhelming.

Making Habits Stick

Connecting new habits to existing behaviors is essential to establish a wellness routine. Known as "habit stacking," this technique involves pairing a new action with a well-established one. For instance:

- After brushing your teeth in the morning, take a few minutes to stretch.
- Before drinking the first cup of coffee, drink a glass of water.
- After finishing dinner, take a short walk outside.

By attaching new habits to familiar routines, individuals increase their chances of maintaining consistency, leading to long-term success.

Tracking Progress: Simple Tools for Consistency

Consistency is key to maintaining a wellness routine, and tracking progress is a powerful way to stay accountable. It provides motivation, helps identify patterns, and ensures continued improvement.

Why Tracking Matters

Monitoring wellness habits helps reinforce progress by providing a tangible record of achievements. It also highlights trends and reveals obstacles that may require adjustments. Tracking can be as straightforward or detailed as necessary, depending on individual preferences and goals.

Effective Tracking Methods

Several simple tools can help maintain consistency and momentum:

1. **Journaling**: A wellness journal can record daily habits, emotions, and reflections on progress. Writing down experiences allows for greater self-awareness and provides insights into what works best.

2. **Habit Tracker Apps**: Digital tools like Habitica, Streaks, and MyFitnessPal make it easy to log activities, set reminders, and view progress charts.

3. **Bullet Journals**: Using a bullet journal with habit-tracking pages allows for creative customization while keeping wellness goals in check.

4. **Checklists and Calendars**: Marking off completed habits on a physical or digital calendar can be a satisfying visual representation of consistency.

Celebrating Small Wins

Acknowledging progress, no matter how small, is crucial for maintaining motivation.
Celebrating achievements—whether completing a whole week of hydration goals or successfully sticking to a new bedtime routine—reinforces positive behavior and encourages long-term commitment.

Overcoming Setbacks: How to Get Back on Track When Life Happens

No matter how dedicated one may be, life inevitably presents challenges that can disrupt a wellness routine. Unexpected obligations, illnesses, or shifts in motivation can lead to setbacks, but the key to long-term success is learning how to recover and realign without guilt.

Understanding Setbacks as Part of the Process

Setbacks are not failures; they are a natural part of personal growth. The key to overcoming them lies in viewing them as learning opportunities rather than reasons to give up. Instead of dwelling on missed days or disrupted routines, individuals should focus on their ability to bounce back.

Strategies for Getting Back on Track

1. **Practice Self-Compassion**: It's easy to fall into a cycle of guilt and self-criticism after missing a workout or neglecting a wellness habit. However, being kind to oneself and recognizing that setbacks happen to everyone makes it easier to move forward.

2. **Reassess and Adjust**: Sometimes, setbacks occur because the original plan was too ambitious or unrealistic. Evaluating the existing routine and making necessary modifications can increase sustainability.

3. **Resume with the Next Best Step**: Instead of feeling pressure to "make up" for lost time, simply start again with a manageable action. If regular exercise has lapsed, resuming a 10-minute session rather than jumping back into an intense regimen can ease the transition.

4. **Use a Trigger to Restart**: Setting a reminder, using a motivational quote, or leaning on a supportive friend can provide the needed push to regain momentum.

5. **Recognize Progress Over Perfection**: Long-term success is not about perfection but consistently working toward wellness. Progress should be measured over weeks and months rather than isolated days.

Building Resilience Through Setbacks

Recovering from setbacks strengthens resilience and reinforces commitment to overall well-being. Each time an individual successfully navigates a challenge, they build confidence in their ability to maintain their wellness routine despite obstacles.

Final Thoughts: A Sustainable Approach to Wellness

Building a wellness routine is not about drastic changes but creating sustainable habits that fit into daily life. Starting small, tracking progress, and learning to overcome setbacks provide a foundation for long-term success. Individuals can cultivate a lifestyle that promotes mental and physical well-being by taking consistent, intentional steps.

Instead of striving for perfection, focusing on progress, adaptability, and self-compassion ensures that wellness remains an achievable and fulfilling journey. When practiced consistently, small habits lead to transformative results, allowing individuals to thrive in their pursuit of health and happiness.

Chapter 3: Mastering Stress in a Chaotic World

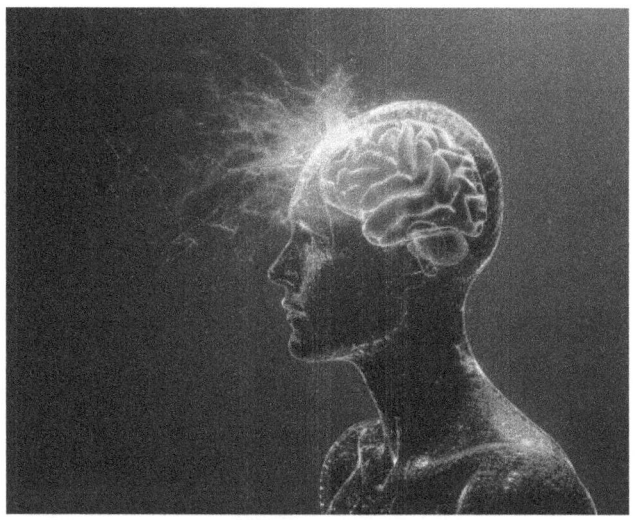

"You don't have to control your thoughts. You just have to stop letting them control you." – Dan Millman

Section 1: Understanding Stress

Stress is an unavoidable aspect of life. Daily responsibilities, significant life changes, and unexpected challenges can trigger it. While stress often carries a negative connotation, it is essential to recognize that not all stress is harmful. Understanding the nature of stress, its long-term effects, and how the body processes it can empower individuals to navigate challenges more effectively and cultivate resilience.

Good Stress vs. Bad Stress: How to Tell the Difference

Stress is not inherently harmful. The body's stress response is a survival mechanism that helps individuals react to danger or demanding situations. However, how stress manifests, and its duration determine whether it has positive or negative consequences.

Eustress: The Positive Side of Stress

Eustress, or "good stress," is a form of stress that enhances motivation, focus, and performance. It provides the push to meet deadlines, prepare for important events, or tackle challenges head-on. Some examples of beneficial stress include:

- Preparing for a big presentation at work or school.
- Training for a competitive event.
- Learning a new skill or taking on a new responsibility.

This type of stress is short-lived and encourages growth and adaptation. It fosters resilience and helps individuals build confidence to handle life's challenges.

Distress: The Harmful Side of Stress

On the other hand, distress, or "bad stress," occurs when stress becomes overwhelming, persistent, or unmanageable. When individuals experience chronic stress without relief, it can lead to emotional, physical, and cognitive exhaustion. Examples of harmful stress include:

- Long-term financial struggles.
- Work-related burnout due to excessive demands and lack of control.
- Relationship conflicts that cause ongoing emotional turmoil.

When stress ceases to be a motivator and instead drains energy, it becomes detrimental to well-being. Understanding the difference between good and bad stress is crucial for developing strategies to mitigate its harmful effects while harnessing its benefits.

The Long-Term Effects of Chronic Stress: What's at Stake

Chronic stress is a persistent state of heightened alertness, often without a clear resolution. Over time, the body and mind suffer from prolonged exposure to stress hormones such as cortisol and adrenaline. The consequences of chronic stress affect nearly every system in the body, from mental health to physical well-being.

Mental and Emotional Consequences

1. **Anxiety and Depression** : Prolonged stress contributes to excessive worry, rumination, and negative thinking patterns. It depletes neurotransmitters responsible for mood regulation, increasing the risk of anxiety disorders and depression.
2. **Cognitive Decline** : Chronic stress impairs concentration, memory, and decision-making. The constant release of stress hormones affects the hippocampus, the brain region responsible for learning and memory.
3. **Emotional Exhaustion** : Long-term stress can result in numbness, irritability, and decreased motivation, making it difficult to engage in daily activities or enjoy life.

Physical Health Risks

1. **Cardiovascular Disease** : High-stress levels increase blood pressure and heart disease risk. Chronic stress may lead to inflammation and arterial damage over time.
2. **Weakened Immune System** : The immune system becomes compromised, making individuals more susceptible to illnesses and infections.
3. **Digestive Issues** : Stress affects gut health, leading to problems

like irritable bowel syndrome (IBS), indigestion, and ulcers.
4. **Sleep Disruptions** : Insomnia and restless sleep are common in individuals with high stress levels, further exacerbating physical and mental health concerns.

Understanding these consequences underscores the importance of managing stress proactively. Identifying chronic stressors and implementing strategies to counteract them can significantly improve overall health and quality of life.

The Stress Response Cycle: How Stress Gets Stuck in Your Body

The human body is designed to respond to stress through a series of physiological reactions that prepare it to confront or escape perceived threats. This is known as the **stress response cycle**, which involves three primary stages: alarm, resistance, and exhaustion.

Stage 1: Alarm Reaction

When a stressor is detected, the body activates the **fight-or-flight** response. The sympathetic nervous system releases adrenaline and cortisol, increasing heart rate, sharpening focus, and directing energy toward immediate action. This response is beneficial in short-term situations, such as avoiding danger or responding to an urgent demand.

Stage 2: Resistance

If the stressor persists, the body remains in a heightened state of alertness. Energy is redirected toward handling the challenge, and physiological responses, such as increased blood pressure and suppressed digestion, continue. While the body attempts to adapt, prolonged exposure to stress hormones begins to take a toll, leading to tension, fatigue, and irritability.

Stage 3: Exhaustion

When stress remains unresolved for an extended period, the body depletes its energy reserves, entering the exhaustion phase. Individuals may experience burnout, emotional fatigue, or physical breakdown at this stage. Symptoms of stress overload include:

- Persistent fatigue and lack of motivation.
- Frequent illness due to a weakened immune system.
- Chronic pain or tension headaches.
- Emotional instability, such as mood swings or withdrawal.

How Stress Gets Stuck in the Body

While the stress response is designed to be temporary, many people experience chronic stress that does not resolve correctly. This happens when the body remains in a constant state of alertness without completing the cycle. Unresolved stress can manifest in several ways:

- **Muscle Tension** : Prolonged stress causes chronic muscle stiffness, particularly in the shoulders, neck, and back.
- **Unreleased Emotions** : Suppressed emotions, such as fear or frustration, can linger and contribute to stress accumulation.
- **Digestive Distress** : The gut-brain connection means stress can lead to digestive problems and gut inflammation.

To effectively complete the stress cycle and restore balance, individuals can engage in activities that signal the body to relax and return to a state of equilibrium. These include:

1. **Physical Movement** : Exercise, stretching, or yoga helps release built-up tension and restore bodily balance.
2. **Deep Breathing** : Slow, controlled breathing activates the parasympathetic nervous system, signaling relaxation.
3. **Social Connection** : Positive social interactions like laughing with friends or receiving support help regulate stress responses.

4. **Creative Expression** : Activities like journaling, painting, or playing music can provide an emotional outlet for unresolved stress.

5. **Rest and Sleep** : Quality sleep allows the body to repair and reset, completing the stress response cycle.

Final Thoughts: A Foundation for Stress Mastery

Understanding stress is the first step in learning to manage it effectively. By differentiating between good and bad stress, recognizing the long-term impact of chronic stress, and understanding the stress response cycle, individuals can take proactive steps to maintain balance.

While stress is inevitable, how we respond to it determines its impact on our well-being. With the proper knowledge and tools, individuals can navigate stress in a way that fosters resilience, growth, and long-term health.

Section 2: Techniques to Manage Stress

Stress is inevitable, but managing it effectively can significantly improve our mental, emotional, and physical well-being. Individuals can build resilience and better navigate stress by incorporating practical techniques such as mindfulness, controlled breathing, and grounding practices. These techniques help shift the body and mind from a heightened stress response, providing clarity even in the most chaotic situations.

Mindfulness Made Simple: Strategies for Staying Present

Mindfulness is being fully present at the moment, without judgment. It allows individuals to acknowledge their thoughts, emotions, and bodily sensations without becoming overwhelmed. Regular mindfulness practice has been shown to reduce stress, improve focus, and enhance overall well-being.

The Benefits of Mindfulness

1. **Reduces Anxiety** : Mindfulness helps prevent overthinking and excessive worry about the future by focusing on the present.

2. **Enhances Emotional Regulation** : Mindfulness encourages self-awareness, allowing individuals to respond to stressors with more significant emotional control.

3. **Improves Concentration** : Practicing mindfulness strengthens attention and cognitive function, making it easier to stay focused amid distractions.

4. **Promotes Relaxation**: Mindfulness activates the parasympathetic nervous system, which counteracts the fight-or-flight response and fosters relaxation.

Simple Mindfulness Techniques

1. **Mindful Breathing** : Pay attention to each inhale and exhale, noticing the sensation of air moving through your nostrils and lungs. If your mind wanders, gently bring your focus back to the breath.

2. **Body Scan Meditation** : Close your eyes and slowly bring awareness to different parts of your body, starting from the toes and moving up to the head. Notice any areas of tension and consciously relax them.

3. **Five-Sense Check-In** : Pause and acknowledge what you are seeing, hearing, smelling, tasting, and feeling in the moment. This simple technique helps ground your awareness in the present.

4. **Gratitude Practice** : Take a few moments each day to reflect on things you are grateful for. This will shift your focus from stress to appreciation, fostering a positive mindset.

5. **Single-Tasking** : Instead of multitasking, focus entirely on one task at a time, whether eating a meal, listening to a conversation, or completing a work assignment.

Practicing mindfulness doesn't require hours of meditation—it can be integrated into daily activities, from washing dishes to walking in nature. The more it is practiced, the more effective it is in reducing stress and promoting inner peace.

Breathing for Calm: Exercises to Reduce Anxiety Quickly

One simplest yet most effective way to manage stress is through conscious breathing. Stress triggers shallow, rapid breathing, which can perpetuate feelings of anxiety. By practicing controlled breathing exercises, individuals can activate the body's relaxation response and restore a sense of calm.

The Science Behind Breathwork

Breathing techniques influence the autonomic nervous system, which regulates stress responses. Deep, slow breathing signals the brain to reduce the production of stress hormones, lower heart rate, and relax muscle tension. This shift helps counteract anxiety and promote mental clarity.

Breathing Exercises to Try

1. **Box Breathing** (Also known as Four-Square Breathing)
    - Inhale through the nose for a count of four.
    - Hold your breath for four seconds.
    - Exhale slowly through the mouth for four seconds.
    - Hold the exhale for another four seconds.
    - Repeat for several cycles to regain control over breathing and reduce stress.
2. **4-7-8 Breathing**
    - Inhale through the nose for a count of four.
    - Hold your breath for a count of seven.
    - Exhale slowly through the mouth for a count of eight.

- This method promotes relaxation and is particularly effective before bedtime.
3. **Diaphragmatic Breathing** (Belly Breathing)
    - Place one hand on the chest and the other on the belly.
    - Inhale deeply through the nose, allowing the belly to expand while keeping the chest still.
    - Exhale slowly through pursed lips, feeling the belly deflate.
    - This technique encourages full oxygen exchange and reduces stress.
4. **Alternate Nostril Breathing** (Nadi Shodhana)
    - Close your right nostril with your thumb and inhale through the left nostril.
    - Close the left nostril with your ring finger and exhale through the right nostril.
    - Inhale through the right nostril, switch sides, and exhale through the left. o   This breathing practice balances the nervous system and calms the mind.

By incorporating these techniques into daily life, individuals can regain control over their physiological responses to stress and cultivate inner stability.

Grounding Practices: Using Your Senses to Find Calm in Chaos

Grounding techniques help anchor individuals in the present moment, especially when stress or anxiety feels overwhelming. By engaging the five senses, grounding techniques provide a tangible way to break the cycle of worry and restore a sense of stability.

Why Grounding Works

When stress triggers a heightened fight-or-flight response, grounding techniques redirect attention away from anxious thoughts and toward the physical world. This shift allows the nervous system to reset and promotes feelings of security and control.

Grounding Techniques to Try

1. **The 5-4-3-2-1 Method**
    - Identify **five things** you can see.
    - Identify **four things** you can touch.
    - Identify **three things** you can hear.
    - Identify **two things** you can smell.
    - Identify **one thing** you can taste.
    - This technique quickly shifts focus away from stress and into the present moment.

2. **Holding a Comfort Object**
    - Holding a small object, such as a smooth stone, fabric, or a stress ball, provides a physical anchor for comfort and stability.

3. **Engaging in Sensory Activities**
    - Walking barefoot on grass, sipping a warm tea, or taking a cool shower can stimulate the senses and ground emotions.

4. **Progressive Muscle Relaxation (PMR)**
    - Tense and relax different muscle groups throughout the body, starting from the toes and working up to the head. This method releases tension and promotes relaxation.

5. **Mindful Observation**
    - Pick an object, such as a flower or a candle flame, and focus on it entirely. Notice its color, shape, texture, and movement to bring awareness into the present moment.

Grounding practices are particularly useful in high-stress situations or moments of panic, offering an immediate way to reclaim calmness and control.

Final Thoughts: A Toolkit for Stress Management

Managing stress effectively requires a combination of mindfulness, breath control, and grounding practices. These techniques provide immediate relief and strengthen long-term resilience to stress. By incorporating these methods into daily life, individuals can cultivate a greater sense of calm, clarity, and balance in an increasingly chaotic world.

With consistent practice, these stress management tools become second nature, allowing individuals to navigate challenges and confidently maintain well-being.

Section 3: Creating Your Stress Toolbox

Stress is unavoidable, but having the right tools can help manage and mitigate its effects. A well-curated stress toolbox provides a variety of strategies for regaining control and calm in different situations. This section explores how to personalize stress management techniques, establish daily stress-busting rituals, and recognize when professional support may be necessary.

Personalizing Your Tools: Finding What Works for You

Each individual responds to stress differently, making it essential to develop a personalized set of coping strategies. What works for one person may not be effective for another. Building a customized stress toolbox involves experimenting with different techniques and identifying which ones provide the most relief.

Assessing Your Stress Responses

To create an effective stress management plan, recognize how stress affects you. Consider the following:

- Do you experience physical symptoms such as headaches or muscle tension?
- Does stress primarily impact your emotions, causing anxiety or irritability?
- Are your thought patterns affected, leading to overthinking or difficulty concentrating?
- You can tailor your coping strategies to address specific needs by identifying your stress responses.

Categories of Stress Management Tools

A well-rounded stress toolbox should include various techniques addressing different stress aspects. These may include:

1. **Physical Strategies**
    - Exercise (e.g., walking, yoga, strength training)
    - Deep breathing exercises
    - Progressive muscle relaxation

2. **Mental and Emotional Strategies**
    - Journaling thoughts and emotions
    - Practicing mindfulness and meditation
    - Engaging in creative activities (e.g., drawing, music, crafts)

3. **Social and Environmental Strategies**
    - Connecting with supportive friends and family
    - Spending time in nature
    - Creating a relaxing environment at home

4. **Lifestyle Adjustments**
    - Prioritizing sleep
    - Maintaining a balanced diet
    - Setting healthy boundaries to prevent burnout

Experimenting and Refining Your Tools

As stressors change, so should your coping techniques. Regularly evaluate your toolbox, noting what continues to work and what may need adjustment. Flexibility in stress management ensures long-term effectiveness and sustainability.

Daily Stress-Busting Rituals: Building Stress Management into Your Routine

Creating a daily routine incorporating stress-reducing activities can help prevent stress from accumulating. Consistency is key to reinforcing and making these habits a natural part of your day.

Morning Rituals to Set a Positive Tone

How you start your day influences your stress levels. Incorporating mindful practices into your morning routine can set a calm and focused foundation.

- **Gratitude Practice:** Take a moment to reflect on what you are thankful for.
- **Stretching or Yoga:** Gentle movement releases tension and prepares the body for the day ahead.
- **Breathwork:** A few minutes of deep breathing can help regulate the nervous system and reduce morning stress.

Midday Strategies for Maintaining Balance

Stress can build throughout the day, making it essential to have tools for maintaining equilibrium.

- **Take Movement Breaks:** Stand up, stretch, or take a short walk to reset your energy.
- **Mindful Eating:** Avoid rushing meals and take the time to savor food mindfully.

- **Check-In with Yourself:** Pause and assess your stress levels to adjust your approach.

Evening Wind-Down Practices

A relaxing nighttime routine helps signal the body that it is time to rest and recover.

- **Limit Screen Time:** Reduce exposure to digital devices at least an hour before bed.
- **Read or Listen to Music:** A calming activity can ease the transition into sleep.
- **Journaling:** Writing thoughts before bed can help process emotions and clear the mind.

Integrating these stress-busting rituals into your day creates a proactive approach to stress management, rather than just reacting to stress when it arises.

Knowing When to Seek Help: Recognizing When You Need Support

While personal stress management tools are valuable, there are times when additional support is necessary. Recognizing when stress becomes unmanageable is crucial for overall well-being.

Signs That Stress is Overwhelming

If stress persists and begins interfering with daily life, it may be time to seek external support. Some key indicators include:

- **Persistent Anxiety or Depression:** Feelings of sadness, hopelessness, or excessive worry that do not improve.
- **Physical Symptoms:** Chronic headaches, digestive issues, or muscle pain without apparent medical cause.
- **Sleep Disruptions:** Difficulty falling asleep or staying asleep due to racing thoughts.

- **Social Withdrawal:** Avoiding social interactions or feeling disconnected from loved ones.
- **Loss of Interest in Activities:** No longer finding joy in hobbies or activities that once provided happiness.

Seeking Professional Help

There is no shame in seeking help from a qualified professional. Therapists, counselors, and medical professionals can provide guidance and interventions tailored to your needs. Options include:

- **Therapy and Counseling:** Speaking with a licensed therapist can help develop coping strategies and process emotions.
- **Support Groups:** Engaging with individuals facing similar challenges can provide encouragement and shared insights.
- **Medical Consultation:** In some cases, stress-related symptoms may require medical intervention, such as medication or specialized treatments.

Building a Support System

Having a network of support can make a significant difference in managing stress. Surrounding yourself with people who uplift and support you fosters emotional resilience. Consider reaching out to:

- Close friends or family members
- Mentors or trusted colleagues
- Community groups or online forums related to stress management

Final Thoughts: Empowering Yourself with a Personalized Toolbox

Building a stress toolbox is a lifelong process that evolves with changing circumstances. By personalizing coping techniques, integrating daily stress-reducing rituals, and recognizing when to seek external support, individuals can develop a comprehensive approach to managing stress effectively.

The key is consistency—slight, intentional daily actions significantly improve overall well-being. Rather than letting stress dictate your life, take proactive steps to build resilience, restore balance, and confidently navigate challenges.

Chapter 4: Emotional Fitness: Mastering Your Inner World

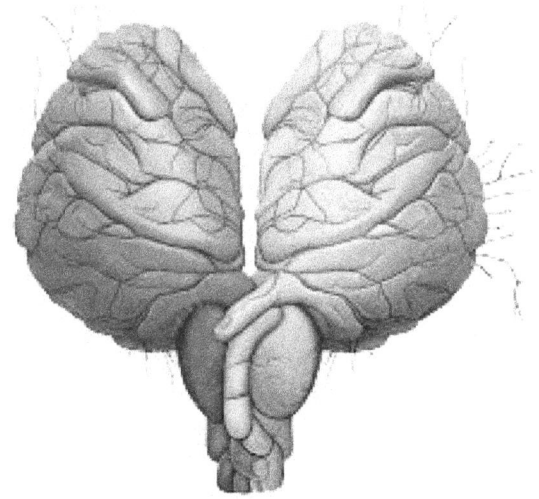

"The mind is everything. What you think you become." – Buddha

Section 1: Understanding Your Emotions

Emotions are an integral part of the human experience. They influence thoughts, behaviors, and overall well-being. Understanding emotions is essential for developing emotional fitness, which is navigating feelings with awareness and control. In this section, we will explore the role of emotions in mental wellness, how to identify and manage emotional triggers, and the connection between thoughts and emotions.

The Role of Emotions in Mental Fitness: Why Emotions Matter

Emotions are more than just fleeting reactions to external events; they are valuable indicators of internal states and experiences. They shape decision-making, relationships, and personal growth. Developing emotional awareness allows individuals to harness emotions as tools for self-improvement rather than obstacles to overcome.

Why Emotions Are Important

1. **Enhancing Self-Awareness** —Recognizing emotions enables individuals to better understand themselves, including their needs, desires, and values.

2. **Influencing Decision-Making** – Emotions play a critical role in making choices. Fear, excitement, joy, and frustration contribute to decisions, from career moves to personal relationships.

3. **Strengthening Relationships** —Emotional intelligence fosters healthy connections with others. Empathy, effective communication of feelings, and appropriate responses enhance relationships in personal and professional settings.

4. **Affecting Physical Health** – Chronic stress, anxiety, and unprocessed emotions can lead to physical health issues, such as high blood pressure, digestive problems, and weakened immune function.

5. **Providing Motivation** – Positive emotions like enthusiasm and passion drive people to pursue goals and aspirations. Negative emotions, such as disappointment, can catalyze change and self-improvement.

Understanding and embracing emotions instead of suppressing them fosters mental resilience. Emotional fitness is about cultivating a balanced approach to emotions—neither avoiding nor being overwhelmed by them.

Emotional Triggers: How to Identify and Manage Them

Emotional triggers are specific events, words, or experiences that elicit strong emotional responses. While some triggers bring about positive emotions, others may cause distress, anger, or anxiety. Identifying and managing these triggers is crucial for emotional stability and personal growth.

Identifying Emotional Triggers

Recognizing what provokes intense emotional reactions requires self-reflection and observation. Some common emotional triggers include:

- **Criticism or Rejection** – Feeling dismissed or unappreciated can trigger self-doubt or insecurity.
- **Unmet Expectations** – Disappointment often arises when reality does not align with personal hopes or beliefs.
- **Past Traumas** – Certain situations or environments may unconsciously remind individuals of painful past experiences.
- **Feeling Ignored or Excluded** – A sense of isolation can trigger feelings of loneliness and frustration.
- **Loss of Control** – Situations that feel unpredictable or out of one's hands can cause anxiety and fear.

To identify personal triggers, individuals can:

- **Observe Reactions** – Pay attention to emotional responses to different situations and people.
- **Reflect on Patterns** – Identify recurring emotions and thoughts linked to specific experiences.
- **Journal Emotions** – Writing down emotional responses provides clarity on what prompts them.
- **Seek Feedback** – Friends, family, or therapists can offer insights into behavioral patterns.

Managing Emotional Triggers

Once emotional triggers are identified, developing strategies for managing them is essential. Some techniques include:

- **Pause and Breathe** – Taking deep breaths before reacting helps create space for thoughtful responses.

- **Reframe the Situation** – Shifting perspective on a triggering event can change its emotional impact.

- **Practice Emotional Regulation Techniques** – Activities like mindfulness, meditation, and grounding exercises can help regulate intense emotions.

- **Communicate Boundaries** – Expressing needs and setting clear boundaries prevents emotional exhaustion.

- **Develop Coping Mechanisms** – Engaging in stress-relieving activities, such as exercise, art, or social support, provides an outlet for processing emotions.

Mastering emotional triggers does not mean eliminating them but instead learning to respond healthily and constructively.

The Mind-Emotion Connection: Thoughts That Drive Feelings

Thoughts and emotions are deeply interconnected. How we think about a situation influences how we feel about it. Understanding this connection allows individuals to develop cognitive strategies that promote emotional balance and well-being.

How Thoughts Influence Emotions

1. **Interpretation Shapes Feelings** – How a person interprets an event determines their emotional response. For example, perceiving a failed exam as a personal failure may lead to feelings of worthlessness while viewing it as a learning opportunity may foster resilience.

2. **Cognitive Distortions Amplify Stress** – Negative thought patterns, such as catastrophizing, black-and-white thinking, or overgeneralization, can intensify emotions unnecessarily.

3. **Beliefs Influence Emotional Reactions** – Core beliefs, formed through past experiences and societal influences, impact how individuals process emotions. Someone who believes they are unworthy of love may react more intensely to rejection.

Techniques to Improve Thought-Emotion Regulation

Developing a balanced mindset requires actively managing thought patterns. Some effective techniques include:

- **Cognitive Reframing** – Challenging and restructuring negative thoughts to promote a healthier perspective.

- **Mindfulness Meditation** – Observing thoughts without judgment reduces emotional reactivity.

- **Gratitude Practice** – Focusing on positive aspects of life enhances overall emotional well-being.

- **Affirmations and Positive Self-Talk** – Replacing self-defeating thoughts with affirmations builds confidence and resilience.

- **Reality Testing** – Questioning the accuracy of negative thoughts helps prevent emotional exaggeration.

Individuals gain control over their emotional landscape by understanding how thoughts influence emotions. The ability to shift perspectives and challenge negative beliefs contributes to emotional mastery and overall mental fitness.

Final Thoughts: Embracing Emotional Awareness for a Balanced Life

Emotional fitness begins with understanding emotions, identifying triggers, and recognizing the powerful connection between thoughts and feelings. By actively working on emotional awareness and regulation, individuals can navigate life's challenges with greater ease and resilience.

Rather than viewing emotions as obstacles, embracing them as valuable signals fosters a deeper understanding of oneself and others. Mastering emotions is not about suppression but about learning to respond rather than react, creating a balanced and fulfilling inner world. Through continuous self-reflection and practice, emotional fitness becomes a lifelong skill that enhances personal growth, relationships, and overall well-being.

Section 2: Tools to Regulate Emotions

Emotions are powerful forces that influence thoughts, behaviors, and interactions with others. Learning to regulate emotions effectively fosters mental resilience and strengthens emotional intelligence. By implementing practical tools like the Pause Technique, Naming and Validating Feelings, and Cognitive Reframing, individuals can develop more outstanding emotional balance and navigate life's challenges with clarity and composure.

The Pause Technique: Stopping Before Reacting

Emotions often trigger automatic responses, sometimes leading to impulsive or regrettable actions. The Pause Technique is a simple yet powerful method that encourages stopping and reflecting before reacting emotionally. This tool is handy in emotionally charged situations where instinctive reactions may escalate conflict or cause unnecessary distress.

Why the Pause Technique Works

1. **Creates Space for Thought** – Taking a moment before reacting allows the rational mind to engage rather than defaulting to an automatic emotional response.

2. **Reduces Emotional Intensity** – Pausing allows emotions to settle, making it easier to respond with clarity rather than heightened intensity.

3. **Enhances Decision-Making** – Instead of acting impulsively, individuals can choose responses that align with their long-term goals and values.

How to Implement the Pause Technique

1. **Recognize the Emotional Surge** – Pay attention to physical and emotional cues that signal a strong reaction, such as increased heart rate, tension, or frustration.

2. **Take a Breath** – Deep breathing helps interrupt the automatic reaction and calms the nervous system.

3. **Count to Five** – Giving the mind a brief pause before responding provides an opportunity to evaluate options.

4. **Ask Yourself Questions** – Consider:
    - "What am I feeling right now?"
    - "What outcome do I want from this situation?"
    - "Is my immediate reaction aligned with my values?"

5. **Choose a Thoughtful Response** – Instead of reacting emotionally, opt for a measured and intentional response that promotes resolution rather than conflict.

The Pause Technique regularly strengthens emotional self-control and fosters mindfulness in daily interactions. Over time, it becomes a natural reflex that prevents impulsive, emotional reactions and promotes constructive communication.

Naming and Validating Feelings: The Power of Acknowledgment

One of the most effective ways to regulate emotions is to acknowledge them openly. Many individuals struggle with emotions because they suppress or ignore them. Naming and validating feelings brings emotions into conscious awareness, allowing for better management and self-understanding.

The Importance of Naming Emotions

1. **Enhances Emotional Clarity** – Naming an emotion helps identify what is experienced rather than feeling overwhelmed.

2. **Reduces Emotional Intensity** – Studies show that labeling emotions can lower their intensity and prevent them from escalating.

3. **Strengthens Emotional Intelligence** – Understanding emotions improves self-awareness and empathy in interpersonal relationships.

How to Name and Validate Feelings

1. **Identify the Emotion** – Ask yourself:
    - "What am I feeling right now?"
    - "Is it anger, sadness, frustration, anxiety, or something else?"
    - "What triggered this feeling?"

2. **Express the Emotion** – Verbalizing the emotion by speaking it aloud or writing it in a journal helps externalize and process the feeling.

3. **Avoid Judgment** – Instead of labeling emotions as "good" or "bad," acknowledge them as natural responses to experiences.

4. **Validate the Emotion** – Recognizing that emotions are valid, even uncomfortable, is essential. Tell yourself:

- "It makes sense that I feel this way, given the situation."
- "My emotions are valid, and I don't need to suppress them."

5. **Consider the Next Step** —Once an emotion is acknowledged, determine whether further action is needed or whether simply recognizing it is enough.

By regularly naming and validating feelings, individuals cultivate emotional awareness and resilience. This practice also fosters a healthier relationship with emotions, reducing the tendency to suppress or ignore critical emotional cues.

Cognitive Reframing: Changing How You See the Situation

Emotions are heavily influenced by perception. The way an individual interprets a situation directly impacts their emotional response. Cognitive reframing shifts perspective to see a problem more constructively or neutrally. This technique is particularly helpful in managing stress, anxiety, and frustration.

How Cognitive Reframing Works

1. **Identifies Thought Patterns** – Recognizing automatic negative thoughts that contribute to emotional distress.
2. **Challenges the Thought** – Evaluating whether the thought is rational or influenced by cognitive distortions.
3. **Creates a Balanced Perspective** – Shifting the interpretation of the situation to one that is more constructive and empowering.

Steps to Apply Cognitive Reframing

1. **Recognize Automatic Negative Thoughts** – Notice when thoughts become extreme, exaggerated, or irrational. Common cognitive distortions include:

- **Catastrophizing** – Assuming the worst possible outcome.
- **Black-and-White Thinking** – Viewing situations in absolutes (e.g., "I failed; therefore, I am a failure").
- **Overgeneralization** – Applying one negative experience to all similar situations.

2. **Question the Validity of the Thought** – Ask yourself:
   - "Is this thought based on facts or assumptions?"
   - "Would I think this way if I were calm and objective?"
   - "What evidence contradicts this thought?"

3. **Reframe the Thought** – Replace the negative thought with a balanced, realistic one.

   For example:
   - Instead of: "I'll never be good at this."
   - Reframe to: "I'm still learning, and improvement takes time."
   - Instead of: "This situation is a disaster."
   - Reframe to: "This is challenging, but I can handle it."

4. **Practice Positive Self-Talk** – Encouraging, supportive language fosters a healthier emotional response to situations. Remind yourself:
   - "I have handled difficulties before and can do it again."
   - "This is just one moment; it does not define me."

5. **Apply Perspective-Taking** – Consider how someone else might view the situation or what advice you would give a friend experiencing the same issue.

By practicing cognitive reframing, individuals gain control over their emotional responses by changing how they perceive challenges. Over time, this technique rewires the brain to focus on constructive and balanced interpretations rather than reactive and distressing thoughts.

Final Thoughts: Strengthening Emotional Regulation

Mastering emotional regulation requires awareness, practice, and patience. The Pause

Technique, Naming and Validating Feelings, and Cognitive Reframing provide powerful tools for navigating emotions effectively. By consistently implementing these techniques, individuals develop excellent emotional fitness, resilience, and overall well-being.

Emotions are not obstacles to be suppressed; they are valuable signals guiding us through life. By managing emotions thoughtfully, individuals can respond to challenges with clarity, maintain healthier relationships, and cultivate inner peace in an ever-changing world.

Section 3: Building Emotional Resilience

Emotional resilience is adapting to challenges, recovering from setbacks, and growing through adversity. It enables individuals to navigate life's ups and downs confidently, maintain a positive outlook, and sustain mental and emotional well-being. Building emotional resilience is a lifelong practice that involves breaking free from negative thought patterns, fostering gratitude and optimism, and transforming setbacks into opportunities for growth.

Letting Go of Negative Patterns: Breaking Free from Ruminations

Negative thought patterns and ruminations can trap individuals in cycles of anxiety, stress, and self-doubt. These persistent thoughts often amplify problems, distort reality, and inhibit emotional growth. Letting go of these harmful patterns is crucial to building emotional resilience.

Recognizing Negative Thought Patterns

1. **Overgeneralization** – Viewing a single negative experience as a pattern that applies to all similar situations (e.g., "I always fail at this.")

2. **Catastrophizing** – Imagining the worst possible outcome and assuming it will happen (e.g., "If I make a mistake, everyone will think I'm incompetent.")

3. **Personalization** – Taking responsibility for events outside of one's control (e.g., "If my friend is upset, it must be because of something I did.")

4. **All-or-Nothing Thinking** – Seeing things in black and white with no room for nuance (e.g., "If I'm not perfect, I must be a failure.")

Strategies to Break Free

1. **Challenge the Thoughts** – Ask yourself:
   - "Is this thought based on facts or assumptions?"
   - "What would I say to a friend experiencing this same thought?"

2. **Reframe the Narrative** – Shift your perspective to a more balanced view:
   - Instead of "I'll never succeed," reframe to "I may have setbacks, but I can learn and improve."

3. **Practice Mindfulness** – Focus on the present moment rather than dwelling on past mistakes or worrying about the future.

4. **Engage in Healthy Distractions** —Activities such as exercise, reading, or taking up a hobby can help break cycles of negative thinking.

5. **Develop Self-Compassion** – Treat yourself with kindness and remind yourself that making mistakes is part of being human.

Letting go of negative thought patterns requires practice, but over time, individuals gain greater control over their thoughts, leading to improved emotional well-being and resilience.

Practicing Gratitude and Optimism: How They Reshape Your Brain

Cultivating gratitude and optimism has a profound impact on emotional resilience. These practices train the brain to focus on positive experiences, fostering a mindset that embraces hope and possibility even in difficult times.

The Science Behind Gratitude and Optimism

Research in neuroscience shows that practicing gratitude and optimism strengthens neural pathways associated with positive thinking and emotional regulation. Gratitude activates the brain's reward system, releasing dopamine and serotonin, which enhance mood and motivation. Optimism fosters cognitive flexibility, allowing individuals to view challenges as temporary and surmountable rather than insurmountable obstacles.

Ways to Cultivate Gratitude

1. **Keep a Gratitude Journal** – Write down three things you are grateful for daily.
2. **Express Appreciation** – Verbally acknowledge and thank others for their kindness and support.

    Reframe Negative Experiences – Identify lessons or silver linings within challenging situations.

    4. **Engage in Acts of Kindness** – Helping others reinforces gratitude and strengthens social connections.

Practicing Optimism

1. **Visualize Positive Outcomes** – Imagine achieving goals and succeeding in future endeavors.

2. **Use Positive Affirmations** – Repeat statements that reinforce self-worth and confidence (e.g., "I am capable and strong.")

3. **Limit Negative Input** – Reduce exposure to pessimistic news or individuals who perpetuate negativity.

4. **Adopt a Growth Mindset** – View failures as learning opportunities rather than permanent setbacks.

By consistently practicing gratitude and optimism, individuals reshape their brain's response to challenges, enhancing their ability to remain resilient and hopeful during adversity.

Turning Setbacks into Growth: Building Confidence in Hard Times

Resilient individuals don't just bounce back from hardships—they grow stronger because of them. Viewing setbacks as opportunities for learning and personal development fosters confidence and adaptability, key components of emotional resilience.

Reframing Setbacks as Opportunities

1. **Acknowledge the Setback** – Accept that difficulties are a natural part of life rather than a personal failure.

2. **Identify Lessons Learned** —Reflect on what the experience taught you about yourself, your strengths, and your areas for growth.

3. **Shift Focus to Solutions** – Instead of dwelling on the problem, consider actionable steps to move forward.

4. **Celebrate Progress** – Recognize small victories, even if they seem minor.

Building Confidence Through Challenges

1. **Resilience in Action** – Facing and overcoming difficulties builds confidence in one's ability to handle future obstacles.

2. **Embracing Discomfort** – Stepping outside of comfort zones fosters personal growth and adaptability.

3. **Developing Self-Efficacy** – Confidence grows when individuals see themselves successfully navigating hardships and becoming more assertive.

4. **Seeking Support When Needed** – Turning to friends, mentors, or therapists for guidance can provide new perspectives and encouragement.

Success Stories of Resilience

- **J.K. Rowling** – Rejected multiple times before publishing *Harry Potter*, demonstrating persistence in adversity.

- **Thomas Edison** – Viewed his thousands of failed attempts at inventing the light bulb as steps toward success.

- **Oprah Winfrey** – Overcame significant personal struggles to become one of the most influential figures in media.

Every setback contains the seeds of growth. Those who embrace challenges as learning experiences develop an unshakable confidence that sustains them through life's uncertainties.

Final Thoughts: Strengthening Emotional Resilience for Life

Building emotional resilience is an ongoing process that involves breaking free from negative thought patterns, fostering gratitude and optimism, and turning setbacks into opportunities for growth. By practicing these skills regularly, individuals cultivate inner strength, adaptability, and confidence in their ability to handle life's challenges.

Resilient individuals embrace adversity as a means of personal transformation rather than fearing it. Emotional resilience empowers people to navigate difficulties with a sense of purpose, maintain a positive perspective, and emerge stronger from every experience. As resilience grows, so does emotional well-being, leading to a more balanced, fulfilling, and empowered life.

Chapter 5: Reconnecting with Your Purpose

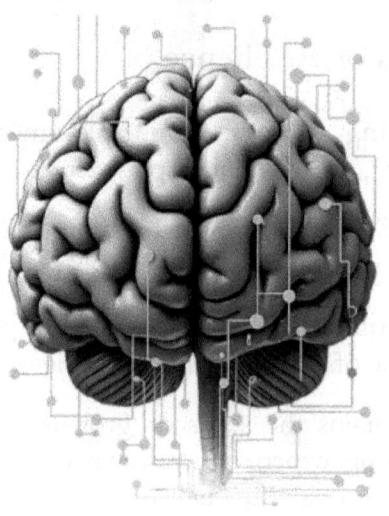

"Your present circumstances don't determine where you can go; they merely determine where you start." – Nido Qubein

Section 1: Finding Clarity in Midlife

Midlife is often a period of deep reflection and transformation. Many individuals question the trajectory of their lives, wondering whether they are truly aligned with their values and purpose. This phase presents an opportunity to transition from living on autopilot to embracing intentionality. By reassessing priorities and recognizing what no longer serves them, individuals can create a more meaningful and fulfilling path forward.

The Midlife Transition: Moving from Autopilot to Intentionality

For many, midlife is when long-held routines and responsibilities feel monotonous or unfulfilling. Years of focusing on career, family, and external expectations may have led to disconnection from personal desires and aspirations. The midlife transition is an invitation to break free from autopilot and embrace a more intentional approach to life.

Signs You May Be on Autopilot

- Feeling unfulfilled despite external success.
- Lacking enthusiasm for activities that once brought joy.
- Experiencing restlessness or a vague sense that something is missing.
- Making decisions based on habit rather than conscious choice.

Shifting Toward Intentionality

1. **Cultivate Self-Awareness** – Take time to reflect on what brings meaning and satisfaction. Journaling or meditation can help uncover desires that have been buried under obligations.
2. **Set Clear Intentions** – Define what matters most and consciously align daily actions with these values.
3. **Embrace Curiosity** – View midlife as a phase of exploration rather than stagnation. Trying new experiences can rekindle passion and provide clarity.
4. **Slow Down** – Rushing through life prevents deep reflection. Intentionality requires moments of stillness to recognize what truly resonates.

Transitioning from autopilot to intentional living is an ongoing process that requires patience and self-compassion. Individuals can move toward a more authentic and purposeful life with time and effort.

Reassessing Your Priorities: Aligning Life with Your Values

At midlife, priorities often shift. What once seemed important—career success, material wealth, societal approval—may no longer feel as meaningful. This phase provides an opportunity to reassess personal values and realign life accordingly.

Understanding Your Core Values

Values serve as internal compasses that guide decision-making and behavior. When life aligns with one's values, there is a sense of coherence and fulfillment. Shared core values include:

- **Family and Relationships** – Prioritizing deep connections and meaningful interactions.
- **Health and Well-being** – Committing to physical, mental, and emotional well-being.
- **Creativity and Growth** – Seeking opportunities for personal and professional development.
- **Service and Contribution** – Making a difference in the lives of others.
- **Freedom and Autonomy** – Valuing independence and the ability to make choices that reflect personal desires.

Steps to Realign Priorities

- **Reflect on What Matters Most** – Consider past decisions and whether they align with current values.
- **Let Go of Societal Expectations** – Recognize the difference between personal desires and external pressures.
- **Make Time for What Matters** – Shift energy and resources toward activities that align with core values.
- **Set Boundaries** – Protect time and energy by saying no to

commitments that no longer serve personal growth.

Reassessing priorities is not about making drastic changes overnight but rather about gradually realigning actions with what truly matters. This process fosters a greater sense of fulfillment and direction.

Recognizing What No Longer Serves You: Letting Go of Old Stories

As people grow, they often hold onto beliefs, habits, and relationships that no longer support their well-being. Midlife is an ideal time to examine these patterns and let go of what no longer serves a positive purpose.

Identifying Outdated Beliefs

Many individuals carry beliefs instilled in them during childhood or early adulthood that may no longer be relevant. These might include:

- "Success is defined by status and wealth."
- "I must always put others before myself."
- "Change is too risky at this stage in life."

Questioning these beliefs and replacing them with perspectives that align with current values allows for growth and renewed purpose.

Letting Go of Toxic Patterns

- **Negative Self-Talk** – Replace critical inner dialogue with self-compassion.
- **Unhealthy Relationships** – Surround yourself with people who uplift and support your growth.
- **Fear-Based Decision-Making** – Take risks that align with your desires rather than avoiding change due to fear.
- **Overcommitment** – Learn to prioritize self-care over obligations that drain energy.

Practical Ways to Release What No Longer Serves You

1. **Practice Mindfulness** – Being present helps identify habits and beliefs that cause distress.
2. **Seek Support** – Working with a coach, therapist, or mentor can guide you in letting go.
3. **Declutter Your Life** – Simplify your environment by removing physical and emotional clutter.
4. **Celebrate Growth** – Acknowledge progress and honor the courage it takes to make changes.

Letting go is not about erasing the past but creating space for new opportunities and experiences that align with a renewed sense of purpose.

Final Thoughts: Embracing Clarity in Midlife

Midlife is not a crisis—it is an opportunity for transformation. By moving from autopilot to intentionality, reassessing priorities, and letting go of what no longer serves them, individuals can reconnect with their purpose and create a more fulfilling future. Clarity comes not from having all the answers but from making conscious choices that reflect personal values and aspirations. This journey toward intentional living allows for growth, joy, and a more profound sense of meaning in the years ahead.

Section 2: Discovering Your "Why"

Finding a sense of purpose is a crucial component of living a fulfilling and meaningful life. When individuals are clear about their "why"—the deeper reason behind their actions and choices—they gain a renewed sense of direction and motivation. This section explores how to reflect on meaningful moments, create a life vision, and take small, intentional steps toward living in alignment with that purpose.

Reflecting on Meaningful Moments: Identifying What Truly Matters

To discover your "why," it is essential to look back at experiences that have brought you fulfillment, joy, or a sense of significance. Meaningful moments often provide clues to what genuinely matters and what contributes to a sense of purpose.

Questions to Reflect On:

1. **When have you felt most fulfilled?** – Consider moments when you felt delighted, engaged, and connected.

2. **What activities make time feel effortless?** – These experiences often point to passions that align with your purpose.

3. **Who inspires you, and why?** – Identifying qualities in others you admire may provide insight into your core values.

4. **What challenges have shaped you?** – Personal struggles and obstacles often lead to meaningful growth and can serve as a foundation for helping others.

5. **What contributions make you feel valued?** – Understanding where you have made a difference in the lives of others can help clarify your purpose.

Extracting Insights from Reflection

After reflecting on these questions, patterns will likely emerge. For example, if your most meaningful moments involve teaching or mentoring others, your purpose may be linked to guiding people toward growth. If creating or problem-solving excites you, your "why" may involve innovation and making a tangible impact. Analyzing these patterns helps form a clearer understanding of what truly matters.

Creating a Life Vision: Designing Your Ideal Future

Once meaningful moments are identified, the next step is envisioning a future that aligns with your purpose. A life vision is a blueprint for making choices that support long-term fulfillment and personal satisfaction.

Building Your Vision Statement

A personal vision statement helps articulate the life you want to create. Consider the following areas when crafting your vision:

1. **Career and Contributions** – What work excites you and allows you to make a meaningful impact?

2. **Relationships and Connections** – What relationships and communities do you want to cultivate?

3. **Health and Well-being** – How do you want to care for your body and mind?

4. **Personal Growth** – What skills, knowledge, or experiences do you want to gain?

5. **Legacy and Impact** – What do you want to be remembered for?

An example of a vision statement might be: *"I want to inspire and empower others through education and mentorship, fostering a supportive and inclusive community that encourages lifelong learning and growth."*

Visualizing Your Ideal Life

To strengthen your vision, mentally immerse yourself in what achieving your purpose looks and feels like. Imagine waking up each morning excited about the life you are creating. What are you doing? Who are you surrounded by? How do you feel? This exercise makes the vision more tangible and inspiring.

Setting Long-Term and Short-Term Goals

To bridge the gap between vision and reality, set both long-term and short-term goals:

- **Long-Term Goals:** Broader objectives that align with your purpose, such as writing a book, launching a nonprofit, or building a fulfilling career in a meaningful field.

- **Short-Term Goals:** Actionable steps that bring you closer to those objectives, such as taking relevant courses, networking with mentors, or setting aside time for passion projects.

A life vision is a guiding star, but it should remain flexible. Life changes, and so too will priorities. Regularly revisiting and adjusting the vision ensures alignment with what feels most meaningful.

The Power of Small Steps: Aligning Daily Actions with Your Purpose

While a life vision provides direction, purpose is ultimately lived through daily actions—small, consistent steps compound over time, leading to significant transformation. Even minor changes in daily habits can reinforce alignment with one's purpose.

Breaking Down the Journey

1. **Identify Key Habits** —Determine habits that align with your purpose. Dedicating time to mentorship or personal development might be beneficial if your goal is to empower others.

2. **Prioritize Small Wins** – Celebrate progress, no matter how small. Completing a single step each day builds momentum.

3. **Develop a Morning Ritual** – Starting the day with intention, such as journaling, exercising, or reading, reinforces a mindset of purpose.

4. **Schedule Purpose-Driven Activities** – Incorporate purpose-related activities into your routine. Whether volunteering,

learning, or creating, make time for what matters.

5. **Reflect and Adjust** – Regularly evaluate your actions to ensure they align with your values and goals.

Overcoming Resistance and Doubt

It's common to encounter self-doubt or external pressures that challenge one's pursuit of purpose. Strategies for staying on track include:

- **Reaffirming Your Why** – Regularly remind yourself of why your purpose matters.

- **Seeking Accountability** – Share goals with a trusted friend or mentor who can provide encouragement and support.

- **Practicing Self-Compassion** – Acknowledge that setbacks are part of growth and focus on progress rather than perfection.

- **Staying Curious** – Purpose evolves; exploring new interests and opportunities ensures continued alignment with what brings fulfillment.

Final Thoughts: Living with Purpose Every Day

Discovering your "why" is not about finding a singular, fixed purpose—it's about continuously aligning life with what brings meaning and fulfillment. Individuals can cultivate a gratifying life by reflecting on meaningful moments, creating a compelling life vision, and taking small but consistent steps.

The journey toward purpose is ongoing and shaped by experiences, relationships, and personal growth. Embracing curiosity, flexibility, and intentionality ensures that each day contributes to a significant life aligned with one's core values. Through conscious effort and commitment, living with purpose becomes an aspiration and a reality.

Section 3: Living with Intention

Living with intention means making conscious choices that align with your values and aspirations. It requires prioritizing what truly matters, fostering a fulfilling life rooted in joy and connection, and staying focused despite inevitable distractions. By embracing intentionality, individuals can create a meaningful and purpose-driven existence.

Prioritizing What Matters Most: Strategies for Saying No

One of the most challenging aspects of intentional living is learning to say no. Many people struggle with obligations that drain their time and energy, disconnecting them from their more profound purpose. Prioritizing what matters most requires setting boundaries and making deliberate choices about how time and resources are spent.

Why Saying No is Essential

- **Protects Energy and Time** – When commitments align with your values, you feel energized rather than depleted.
- **Reduces Stress and Overwhelm** – Overcommitting leads to burnout, making it difficult to focus on what truly matters.
- **Enhances Relationships** – Being selective with time allows for deeper, more meaningful connections.
- **Supports Personal Growth** – Saying no to distractions makes space for personal and professional development.

Strategies for Saying No Gracefully

1. **Clarify Your Priorities** – Before committing to anything, ask yourself:
    - Does this align with my values?

- Will this bring me closer to my goals?
- Am I doing this out of obligation or genuine desire?

2. **Use a Decision-Making Framework** – Employ the "Hell Yes or No" rule—if an opportunity doesn't excite you, decline it.

3. **Set Firm Boundaries** – Communicate limits. For example:
    - "I appreciate the opportunity but can't commit to this right now."
    - "I need to focus on my current priorities, so I won't be able to participate."

4. **Delegate When Possible** – If a request is necessary but not essential for you to handle personally, consider passing it on to someone else.

5. **Practice Saying No with Confidence** – Rehearse responses in advance to ease discomfort.

6. **Offer Alternatives** —Instead of outright refusal, suggest another solution, such as rescheduling or contributing differently.

By effectively learning to say no, individuals free themselves from unnecessary obligations and create space for what enriches their lives.

Building a Life of Fulfillment: How to Focus on Joy and Connection

Fulfillment comes from engaging in activities that bring joy, meaning, and connection. While external achievements often measure success, true satisfaction is rooted in how life feels internally. Cultivating fulfillment requires intentional choices that nurture happiness and relationships.

The Key Elements of a Fulfilling Life

1. **Joy in Everyday Moments** – Happiness is found in small, daily experiences, not just grand accomplishments.

2. **Authentic Relationships** – Deep connections with family, friends, and community foster emotional well-being.

3. **Purposeful Work** – Engaging in meaningful activities—whether through career, hobbies, or volunteerism—enhances life satisfaction.

4. **Gratitude and Mindfulness** – Appreciating the present moment leads to greater contentment.

5. **Personal Growth** – Continuously learning and evolving keeps life fulfilling and engaging.

Practical Ways to Cultivate Joy and Connection

1. **Identify What Brings You Joy** – List activities that make you feel alive and prioritize them.

2. **Schedule Meaningful Experiences** – Make time for hobbies, nature, and spontaneous adventures.

3. **Strengthen Relationships** – Invest in deepening bonds with loved ones through quality time, active listening, and shared experiences.

4. **Practice Gratitude Daily** – Reflecting on positive aspects of life fosters a greater sense of fulfillment.

5. **Create Rituals for Well-Being** – Establish habits such as morning meditation, journaling, or weekly gatherings with loved ones.

A fulfilling life is not about chasing external milestones but curating daily experiences that bring genuine happiness and meaning.

Staying True to Your Purpose: Overcoming Distractions

Internal and external distractions can pull individuals away from their purpose. Focusing on what truly matters requires conscious effort in a world filled with obligations, digital temptations, and societal expectations.

Common Distractions That Derail Purpose

- **Social Media and Technology** – Excessive screen time can lead to mindless consumption rather than meaningful engagement.

- **People-Pleasing** – Saying yes to everything dilutes energy and focus.

- **Fear and Self-Doubt** – Internal doubts and fear of failure can hinder progress.

- **Lack of Clear Goals** – Without direction, it's easy to drift aimlessly.

Strategies to Stay Focused on Purpose

1. **Define Clear Intentions** – Write down what truly matters and revisit it regularly.

2. **Create a Distraction-Free Environment** – Minimize interruptions by setting boundaries around work and personal time.

3. **Limit Time on Low-Value Activities**—Track time spent and reduce engagement in activities that don't add value.

4. **Develop a Daily Purpose Ritual** – Begin each morning by setting an intention for the day.

5. **Surround Yourself with Supportive People** – Engage with individuals, encouraging growth and accountability.

6. **Manage Fear and Doubt** – Recognize that setbacks are part of the journey and use them as learning experiences.

Individuals can maintain momentum and continue living with intention by actively reducing distractions and staying committed to purposeful actions.

Final Thoughts: Embracing an Intentional Life

Living with intention is about making choices that align with personal values, bring joy, and sustain meaningful connections. Individuals can cultivate a life rich in purpose and authenticity by prioritizing what truly matters, focusing on fulfillment, and staying committed despite distractions.

Intentional living is not about perfection but about conscious effort. No matter how small, each decision contributes to a greater sense of alignment and well-being. Through daily mindfulness, clear priorities, and consistent action, anyone can create a gratifying and purpose-driven life.

Chapter 6: Strengthening Connections: Relationships That Uplift

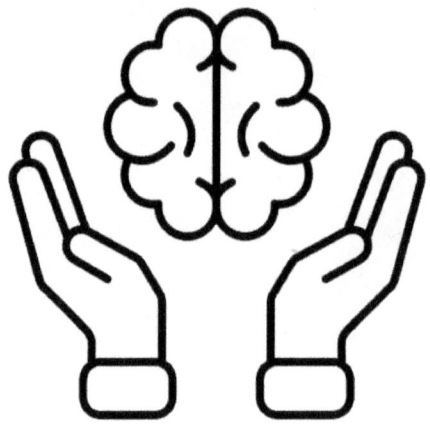

"Do the best you can until you know better. Then when you know better, do better." – Maya Angelou

Section 1: The Power of Social Connection

Human beings are inherently social creatures. Our relationships shape our emotional well-being, influence our daily experiences, and provide a foundation for a fulfilling life. In this section, we explore the science behind why relationships impact mental health, how to recognize toxic patterns that drain us and the role of the community in building a strong support network.

Why Relationships Impact Mental Health: The Science of Connection

Research consistently shows that strong social connections are essential for emotional and mental well-being. Relationships with friends, family, colleagues, or community members contribute significantly to happiness and resilience.

The Neuroscience of Connection

1. **Oxytocin and Bonding:** Positive social interactions release oxytocin, often called the "love hormone," which fosters trust, reduces stress, and strengthens emotional bonds.

2. **Dopamine and Reward:** Engaging in meaningful connections activates the brain's reward system, releasing dopamine and contributing to feelings of joy and motivation.

3. **Cortisol and Stress Reduction:** Supportive relationships lower cortisol levels, the primary stress hormone, reducing the risk of anxiety and depression.

4. **Mirror Neurons and Empathy:** Our brains are wired to reflect the emotions of those around us, enhancing empathy and deepening connections.

Emotional and Physical Benefits of Strong Relationships

- **Reduced Risk of Depression and Anxiety:** Those with strong social ties report lower levels of mental distress.

- **Improved Longevity:** Studies show that individuals with strong relationships live longer and enjoy better physical health.

- **Greater Resilience:** A support network helps navigate life's challenges, from job loss to personal struggles.

- **Enhanced Self-Worth:** Being part of a supportive group reinforces a sense of belonging and purpose.

Prioritizing meaningful relationships is a crucial component of overall well-being. However, not all relationships are beneficial. Identifying and addressing toxic patterns is equally essential.

Recognizing Toxic Patterns: Identifying Relationships That Drain You

While healthy relationships uplift and energize, toxic ones do the opposite, leading to stress, self-doubt, and emotional exhaustion. Recognizing unhealthy patterns allows individuals to set boundaries and cultivate relationships that foster growth and well-being.

Signs of a Toxic Relationship

1. **Constant Negativity:** If a relationship consistently leaves you feeling drained, anxious, or undervalued, it may be toxic.

2. **Lack of Reciprocity:** Healthy relationships involve mutual care and support. One-sided relationships can lead to burnout and resentment.

3. **Manipulation and Control:** Red flags are emotional manipulation, guilt-tripping, or controlling behavior.

4. **Excessive Criticism:** Constructive feedback is essential, but constant belittling or undermining erodes self-esteem.

5. **Jealousy and Possessiveness:** A supportive friend or partner encourages personal growth rather than restricting it.

6. **Unreliability and Broken Trust:** Frequent dishonesty or inconsistency weakens trust and security in any relationship.

How to Address Toxic Relationships

- **Set Clear Boundaries:** Communicate your needs and limits openly.

- **Limit Exposure:** Reduce time spent with individuals who consistently drain your energy.

- **Seek Support:** Confide in trusted friends or a therapist to gain perspective.

- **Practice Self-Compassion:** Letting go of toxic relationships can be difficult, but prioritizing well-being is essential.

- **End the Relationship If Necessary:** In cases of severe emotional harm, stepping away from the relationship may be the healthiest choice.

Recognizing and addressing toxic relationships creates space for healthier connections that contribute to a sense of security, joy, and fulfillment.

The Role of Community: Finding Your Support Network

Beyond individual relationships, the larger community plays a vital role in emotional well-being. A strong support network provides encouragement, shared experiences, and a sense of belonging.

Why Community Matters

1. **Emotional Support:** Being part of a community means having people to turn to in need.

2. **Shared Identity and Purpose:** Groups with common interests and values foster a sense of belonging.

3. **Increased Accountability:** Whether in health, career, or personal growth, community support encourages consistency and motivation.

4. **Opportunities for Growth:** Exposure to diverse perspectives within a community enriches learning and development.

How to Find and Build Your Support Network

- **Engage in Shared Interests:** Join clubs, volunteer groups, or professional organizations that align with your passions.

- **Prioritize Face-to-Face Interactions:** While online connections are valuable, in-person interactions foster deeper bonds.

- **Be Open to Vulnerability:** Meaningful relationships grow through authenticity and shared experiences.

- **Give as Much as You Receive:** Support networks thrive when members actively contribute and uplift one another.

- **Cultivate Relationships Across Different Areas:** A mix of personal, professional, and community connections provides well-rounded support.

Strengthening Existing Community Ties

- **Reconnect with Old Friends:** Reach out to past friends and acquaintances who align with your values.

- **Deepen Family Bonds:** Strengthening family relationships fosters a stable emotional foundation.

- **Attend Local Events:** Participating in neighborhood gatherings or cultural events helps forge new connections.

- **Engage in Acts of Service:** Helping others strengthens community ties and provides a sense of purpose.

A strong, supportive community enhances resilience, promotes well-being, and provides encouragement in both joyful and challenging times.

Final Thoughts: Embracing the Power of Social Connection

The quality of our relationships directly influences our emotional health and overall happiness. Prioritizing strong social connections, setting boundaries in toxic relationships, and finding a supportive community are all essential steps in fostering meaningful connections. By investing in healthy relationships and engaging with supportive networks, individuals create a foundation for a fulfilling and resilient life.

Social connection is not just a luxury but a fundamental pillar of well-being. We pave the way for greater joy, purpose, and emotional balance by cultivating relationships that uplift and energize.

Section 2: Building Better Relationships

Relationships are the foundation of a fulfilling life. Healthy connections provide emotional support and contribute to personal growth and well-being. However, maintaining and improving relationships requires intentional effort. This section explores three fundamental components of building better relationships: communicating, practicing active listening, and setting healthy boundaries.

Communicating with Clarity: How to Express Your Needs Effectively

Effective communication is the cornerstone of any healthy relationship. Whether with a partner, friend, colleague, or family member, expressing needs and emotions fosters understanding and prevents misunderstandings.

Why Clear Communication Matters

- **Prevents Misunderstandings** – There is less room for misinterpretation when thoughts and feelings are clarified.
- **Strengthens Trust** – Honest and transparent conversations build trust and deepen connections.
- **Encourages Healthy Conflict Resolution** – When individuals express themselves without ambiguity, addressing and resolving conflicts becomes easier.
- **Boosts Emotional Connection** – Open communication fosters a sense of security and closeness in relationships.

How to Communicate Clearly

1. **Know What You Want to Say** – Before initiating a conversation, take a moment to clarify your thoughts and emotions.

2. **Use "I" Statements** – Rather than blaming or accusing, frame statements to reflect personal feelings and perspectives (e.g., "I feel overwhelmed when..." instead of "You never help me with...").

3. **Be Specific and Concise** – Avoid vague language. Clearly state what you need or how you feel.

4. **Maintain a Calm Tone** – Emotional regulation is crucial for effective communication. Avoid raising your voice or using aggressive language.

5. **Practice Nonverbal Communication** – Body language, facial expressions, and eye contact play a significant role in receiving messages.

6. **Be Open to Feedback** – Communication is a two-way process. Encourage the other person to share their perspective as well.

Clear and assertive communication nurtures healthy interactions, ensuring that needs and expectations are understood and met.

The Art of Active Listening: Strengthening Bonds with Presence

Listening is just as critical as speaking in any relationship. Active listening demonstrates respect, empathy, and a genuine interest in the other person's experiences and emotions.

Why Active Listening is Essential

- **Enhances Understanding** – Fully engaging with another person's words and emotions allows a more profound comprehension of their needs and concerns.

- **Builds Emotional Intimacy** – Feeling heard and valued strengthens emotional bonds.

- **Reduces Conflict** – Many misunderstandings stem from poor listening. Actively listening minimizes assumptions and unnecessary disputes.

- **Fosters Mutual Respect** – When people feel genuinely heard, they are likelier to reciprocate with attentiveness and empathy.

Steps to Practice Active Listening

1. **Give Full Attention** – Put away distractions like phones and laptops. Maintain eye contact to show engagement.

2. **Practice Reflective Listening** . Repeat the speaker's words to confirm understanding (e.g., "So what I hear you saying is...").

3. **Use Nonverbal Cues** – Nodding, maintaining an open posture, and encouraging expressions show attentiveness.

4. **Avoid Interrupting** – Allow the speaker to finish their thoughts before responding.

5. **Ask Clarifying Questions** – If something is unclear, ask open-ended questions to gain deeper insight.

6. **Validate Feelings** – Acknowledge the other person's emotions by saying things like, "That sounds frustrating" or "I can see why you feel that way."

Active listening strengthens relationships by making people feel valued and understood. When both parties are fully present in conversations, deeper connections are cultivated.

Setting Healthy Boundaries: Protecting Your Peace

Healthy relationships require mutual respect and understanding, which includes respecting personal boundaries. Boundaries help individuals protect their mental, emotional, and physical well-being.

Why Boundaries Are Necessary

- **Prevents Burnout** – Overextending oneself in relationships can lead to emotional exhaustion.
- **Encourages Mutual Respect** – Boundaries set expectations for how individuals wish to be treated.
- **Reduces Resentment** – People are less likely to feel taken advantage of when they honor their needs.
- **Promotes Personal Growth** – Establishing and enforcing boundaries fosters self-respect and self-awareness.

Types of Boundaries

1. **Emotional Boundaries** – Protecting oneself from emotional manipulation or excessive negativity.
2. **Time Boundaries** – Setting limits on time commitments to avoid overcommitment and stress.
3. **Physical Boundaries** – Defining comfort levels for personal space and physical interactions.
4. **Mental Boundaries** – Maintaining autonomy in thoughts, beliefs, and values.
5. **Social Boundaries** – Deciding who to spend time with and which social obligations to accept.

How to Set and Maintain Boundaries

1. **Identify Personal Limits** – Reflect on what makes you feel uncomfortable or drained.
2. **Communicate Clearly** – Express boundaries directly and confidently.
3. **Be Consistent** – Uphold boundaries even when faced with resistance.
4. **Use Assertive Communication** – Politely but firmly say no

when necessary.

5. **Prioritize Self-Care** – Ensure that boundaries support overall well-being.

Examples of setting boundaries:

- **With Work:** "I am unavailable after 7 PM for work-related calls."
- **With Family:** "I appreciate your advice, but I need to decide on my own."
- **With Friends:** "I need to take some time for myself this weekend, but let's catch up next week."

Setting and maintaining boundaries is an act of self-respect. It ensures that relationships remain balanced, mutually supportive, and emotionally healthy.

Final Thoughts: Cultivating Stronger, More Fulfilling Relationships

Building better relationships requires ongoing effort, intentional communication, and mutual respect. Individuals can cultivate more profound, meaningful connections by expressing needs clearly, practicing active listening, and setting healthy boundaries.

Relationships thrive when both parties feel heard, valued, and respected. Implementing these principles fosters trust, strengthens emotional bonds, and contributes to a supportive and fulfilling social environment. As individuals commit to these practices, they create relationships that uplift and provide a foundation for personal growth and emotional well-being.

Section 3: Strengthening Your Inner Circle

Our relationships profoundly shape our lives, influencing our happiness, well-being, and personal growth. A strong inner circle provides support, encouragement, and companionship. However, maintaining and strengthening these meaningful connections requires intentional effort. This section explores investing in quality relationships, nurturing bonds through life changes, and embracing forgiveness as a tool for healing and growth.

Investing in Meaningful Connections: Quality Over Quantity

In today's digital world, equating connection with our number of friends or followers is easy. However, authentic connection isn't about quantity—it's about depth. Having a handful of genuine, supportive relationships is far more valuable than having many surface-level interactions.

Why Quality Matters in Relationships

- **Emotional Support** – Deep connections provide a safe space for vulnerability, offering comfort in times of need.

- **Trust and Reliability** – Strong relationships are built on mutual trust, allowing individuals to rely on one another.

- **Mutual Growth** – Meaningful relationships encourage personal and emotional development.

- **Reduced Stress** – Close, supportive bonds contribute to lower stress levels and improved mental health.

How to Cultivate Quality Relationships

1. **Prioritize Time Together** – Regularly schedule one-on-one time with loved ones through phone calls, coffee dates, or shared activities.

2. **Engage in Deep Conversations** – Move beyond small talk to discuss dreams, struggles, and personal insights.

3. **Show Genuine Interest** – Listen and ask thoughtful questions about the other person's experiences and emotions.

4. **Express Appreciation** – Acknowledge and express gratitude for the presence of meaningful people in your life.

5. **Be Reliable and Trustworthy** – Consistently showing up for others builds stronger, lasting connections.

Strengthening your inner circle means valuing depth and sincerity over social breadth. True friendships and deep connections flourish when nurtured with intention and care.

Nurturing Relationships Through Change: Staying Close During Transitions

Change is an inevitable part of life, and relationships often face challenges during significant transitions. Maintaining close bonds requires adaptability and effort, whether a career shift, a move to a new city, or personal growth.

Common Life Transitions That Impact Relationships

- **Career Changes** – New job demands may lead to less availability, requiring adjustment in communication.

- **Relocation** – Moving to a new place can physically separate individuals from their support networks.

- **Family Changes** – Marriage, parenthood, or caregiving responsibilities can alter relationship dynamics.

- **Personal Growth** – As individuals evolve, relationships must adapt to new perspectives and priorities.

Strategies for Maintaining Strong Bonds During Change

1. **Communicate Openly** – Express your feelings, expectations, and concerns with those closest to you.

2. **Adapt to New Routines** – Find ways to integrate quality time despite shifting schedules.

3. **Utilize Technology** – Stay connected through video calls, messages, and voice notes when physical distance is a barrier.

4. **Respect Growth and Space** – Allow room for personal evolution while reinforcing mutual support.

5. **Create New Traditions** – Find creative ways to stay engaged, such as scheduling regular check-ins or planning visits.

By intentionally nurturing relationships through change, you reinforce the strength and longevity of your inner circle, ensuring that bonds remain intact despite life's inevitable shifts.

The Role of Forgiveness: Letting Go to Move Forward

Forgiveness is an essential element of maintaining strong and healthy relationships. Holding onto resentment or past hurts can create emotional barriers, preventing connections from deepening. Learning to forgive ourselves and others fosters healing and strengthens relationships.

Why Forgiveness Matters in Relationships

- **Restores Trust** – Forgiveness allows for rebuilding trust after misunderstandings or conflicts.

- **Reduces Emotional Burden** – Letting go of grudges alleviates stress and promotes emotional well-being.

- **Encourages Growth** – Forgiveness fosters maturity and personal development.

- **Deepens Emotional Bonds** – Genuine forgiveness strengthens connections by demonstrating resilience and understanding.

Steps Toward Forgiveness

1. **Acknowledge the Hurt** – Recognize and process the emotions tied to the situation.

2. **Understand the Other Perspective** – Empathy can help see

the situation from a broader perspective.

3. **Decide to Forgive** – Forgiveness is a choice that leads to emotional liberation.

4. **Communicate if Necessary** – Express feelings openly when it is helpful for closure.

5. **Release Resentment** – Letting go of past pain creates space for healing and renewed trust.

Self-Forgiveness: An Important Component

Forgiving oneself is equally crucial. Mistakes and missteps are part of the human experience, and self-compassion is necessary for personal growth. By letting go of self-judgment, individuals create healthier relationships with themselves and others.

Forgiveness is not about forgetting or excusing harm but about freeing oneself from the burden of past grievances. It is vital to ensure relationships remain strong, even after moments of conflict.

Final Thoughts: Strengthening the Bonds That Matter

Building and maintaining a strong inner circle requires commitment, communication, and compassion. Individuals can cultivate uplifting, resilient, and deeply fulfilling connections by investing in quality relationships, adapting to change with openness, and practicing forgiveness.

Strong relationships are built on trust, understanding, and shared experiences. When nurtured with care and intention, they become potent sources of support, inspiration, and joy throughout life's journey.

Chapter 7: Thriving in a Digital World

"Almost everything will work again if you unplug it for a few minutes, including you." – Anne Lamott

Section 1: Understanding Digital Overload

The digital world has transformed how we connect, communicate, and consume information. While technology offers immense benefits, excessive digital engagement can lead to mental exhaustion, reduced self-esteem, and emotional distress. Understanding digital overload is crucial for developing a balanced approach to technology use, ensuring that digital tools enhance rather than hinder our well-being.

The Impact of Technology on Mental Health: Pros and Cons of Being Connected

The digital revolution has redefined social interactions, work environments, and entertainment. While technology enhances many aspects of life, overuse can negatively impact mental health.

Pros of Being Connected

1. **Access to Information** – The internet provides instant access to knowledge, learning resources, and global news.

2. **Convenience and Efficiency** – Digital tools simplify daily tasks, from online banking to remote work and education.

3. **Social Connectivity** – Technology helps people stay in touch with friends and family, regardless of geographical distance.

4. **Opportunities for Creativity** – Digital platforms offer avenues for creative expression, including blogging, photography, and music.

5. **Mental Health Support** – Online therapy, mental health apps, and self-help resources support those in need.

Cons of Being Connected

1. **Increased Stress and Anxiety** – Constant notifications, emails, and social media updates create pressure and stress.

2. **Reduced Attention Span** – Excessive digital consumption contributes to difficulty focusing and retaining information.

3. **Sleep Disruptions** – Screen blue light interferes with melatonin production, affecting sleep quality.

4. **Decreased Face-to-Face Interaction** – Over-reliance on digital communication can weaken in-person social skills and relationships.

5. **Overstimulation and Information Overload** – The sheer volume of online content can be overwhelming, leading

to decision fatigue and mental exhaustion.

Balancing technology's advantages while mitigating its negative effects is key to maintaining mental well-being in the digital age.

The Trap of Comparison: How Social Media Affects Self-Esteem

Social media has revolutionized how people interact, share experiences, and seek validation. However, it has also created a culture of comparison that can negatively impact self-esteem and mental health.

Why Social Media Fuels Comparison

1. **Highlight Reels vs. Reality** – People often showcase curated, idealized versions of their lives on social media, creating unrealistic expectations.

2. **Validation Through Likes and Comments** – Pursuing external validation through engagement metrics can lead to self-worth tied to online approval.

3. **Algorithm-Driven Content** – Social media platforms amplify content that evokes strong emotions, including envy and insecurity.

4. **Constant Exposure to "Perfect" Lives** – Seeing influencers, celebrities, and peers seemingly living flawless lives can create a sense of inadequacy.

5. **Fear of Missing Out (FOMO)** – Seeing others enjoy experiences, vacations, or achievements can lead to feelings of exclusion and dissatisfaction.

How to Break Free from the Comparison Trap

1. **Limit Social Media Usage** – Set boundaries for daily screen time and avoid excessive scrolling.

2. **Curate Your Feed** – Unfollow accounts that trigger negative emotions and follow those that promote positivity and

authenticity.

3. **Practice Gratitude** – Shift focus from what's lacking to appreciating personal achievements and experiences.

4. **Engage in Real-Life Interactions** – Prioritize face-to-face connections and hobbies that bring genuine fulfillment.

5. **Remember the Illusion of Perfection** – Recognize that social media presents a filtered reality, not the complete picture.

Individuals can protect their self-esteem and well-being by fostering self-awareness and developing a healthier relationship with social media.

Recognizing Digital Burnout: Signs You Need a Break

Digital burnout is the physical and mental exhaustion caused by excessive screen time and online engagement. Recognizing the symptoms early allows individuals to take proactive steps toward digital well-being.

Signs of Digital Burnout

1. **Mental Fatigue** – Feeling overwhelmed, unfocused, or mentally drained after prolonged screen exposure.

2. **Irritability and Anxiety** – Increased frustration, impatience, or restlessness due to constant notifications and digital demands.

3. **Sleep Disturbances** – Difficulty falling asleep or waking up feeling unrested due to excessive screen exposure before bed.

4. **Physical Symptoms** – Headaches, eye strain, neck pain, and reduced physical activity due to prolonged device use.

5. **Decreased Productivity** – Struggling to complete tasks efficiently due to constant digital distractions.

6. **Social Withdrawal** – Preferring digital interactions over in-person connections or feeling disconnected from loved ones.

7. **Loss of Enjoyment** – No longer enjoying offline activities that once brought joy.

How to Overcome Digital Burnout

1. **Schedule Screen-Free Time** – Implement daily or weekly breaks from digital devices.

2. **Practice Mindful Tech Use** – Be intentional about when and how technology is used.

3. **Prioritize Sleep Hygiene** – Reduce screen exposure before bed and use night mode settings.

4. **Engage in Offline Activities** – Exercise, read a book, or spend time in nature to reset the mind and body.

5. **Unplug Regularly** – Consider a digital detox by taking extended breaks from social media and unnecessary screen time.

6. **Set Boundaries** – Establish limits for checking emails, notifications, and social media.

7. **Use Technology Wisely** – Opt for apps and platforms that enhance well-being rather than deplete energy.

By identifying digital burnout early and implementing strategies to regain balance, individuals can cultivate a healthier relationship with technology and prioritize overall well-being.

Final Thoughts: Embracing a Balanced Digital Life

Technology is a powerful tool that enhances communication, learning, and productivity. However, when overused or mismanaged, it can lead to mental exhaustion, reduced self-esteem, and digital burnout. Individuals can cultivate a healthier, more balanced relationship with the digital world by being mindful of technology's impact, avoiding the comparison trap, and recognizing the signs of burnout.

Thriving in a digital world is not about eliminating technology but using it intentionally. Individuals can harness technology's benefits while safeguarding their mental and emotional well-being by setting boundaries, prioritizing real-world connections, and engaging with digital platforms mindfully.

Section 2: Taking Control of Technology

Managing technology usage is crucial for maintaining mental and emotional well-being in an era dominated by digital interactions. While technology provides unparalleled convenience and connectivity, unchecked screen time and harmful digital environments can lead to stress, anxiety, and decreased productivity. Individuals can foster a balanced and healthy relationship with technology by implementing mindful strategies such as setting screen-time limits, curating a positive digital space, and practicing mindful tech usage.

Setting Screen-Time Limits: Finding Balance in a Connected World

Excessive screen time has been linked to increased stress, reduced focus, and disrupted sleep patterns. Finding the right balance between digital engagement and offline activities is essential for maintaining a healthy lifestyle.

Why Screen-Time Limits Matter

1. **Prevents Digital Burnout** – Spending excessive hours on screens can lead to mental fatigue and reduced productivity.
2. **Improves Sleep Quality** – Exposure to blue light from screens before bedtime disrupts melatonin production, making it harder to fall asleep.
3. **Enhances Real-Life Interactions** – Limiting screen time encourages more profound connections with family, friends, and colleagues.
4. **Boosts Productivity and Focus** – Managing digital

distractions helps improve concentration and task efficiency.

5. **Encourages Physical Activity** – Reducing screen time frees up time for movement, exercise, and outdoor activities.

Strategies for Setting Screen-Time Limits

1. **Use Built-in Screen-Time Tracking Tools** – Most smartphones and computers offer tracking features that provide insights into daily screen usage.

2. **Implement the 20-20-20 Rule** – Every 20 minutes, take a 20-second break to look at something 20 feet away to reduce eye strain.

3. **Create Tech-Free Zones** – Establish areas in your home, such as the bedroom or dining table, where digital devices are not allowed.

4. **Set Digital Curfews** – Avoid screens at least one hour before bedtime to improve sleep quality.

5. **Schedule Offline Activities** – Plan hobbies, workouts, and social outings encouraging screen-free engagement.

6. **Use App Timers and Website Blockers** – Tools like Freedom, StayFocusd, or Apple's Screen Time can help regulate time spent on distracting apps.

By proactively setting screen time limits, individuals can cultivate a healthier relationship with technology, ensuring it enhances rather than detracts from daily life.

Curating a Positive Digital Space: Filtering Out Negativity Online

The digital space can be a source of inspiration and learning or a breeding ground for negativity and stress. Mindfully curating online interactions and content consumption can create a healthier, uplifting digital experience.

How Negative Digital Spaces Affect Mental Well-Being

1. **Exposure to Toxicity** – Constant exposure to negative news, online arguments, or cyberbullying can lead to emotional exhaustion.

2. **Comparison and Self-Doubt** – Social media often presents idealized versions of reality, fueling unrealistic expectations and self-criticism.

3. **Information Overload** – The constant barrage of content can lead to mental fatigue and decision paralysis.

4. **Reduced Productivity** – Engaging with negative or time-consuming online distractions hinders focus and efficiency.

How to Curate a Positive Digital Space

1. **Audit Your Social Media Feed** – Unfollow or mute accounts that provoke stress, comparison, or negativity. Follow individuals and organizations that inspire, educate, and uplift.

2. **Limit Exposure to Negative News** – Stay informed, but avoid excessive consumption of distressing news stories.

3. **Join Supportive Online Communities** – Engage with digital spaces that promote constructive conversations and mutual support.

4. **Practice Digital Minimalism** – Simplify your digital life by unsubscribing from unnecessary email lists and decluttering your social media accounts.

5. **Control Notifications** – Disable non-essential alerts to minimize distractions and regain focus.

6. **Be Intentional with Content Consumption** – Choose podcasts, books, and videos that add value to your knowledge and well-being rather than passively consuming content.

By filtering out negativity and cultivating an intentional digital environment, individuals can ensure that their online experiences contribute positively to their mental and emotional health.

Mindful Tech Usage: Strategies to Stay Present While Staying Connected Technology is a powerful tool, but its constant presence can lead to mindless scrolling, decreased focus, and a weakened ability to engage in the present moment. Practicing mindful tech usage enables individuals to use technology intentionally, ensuring it enhances rather than dominates their lives.

The Importance of Mindful Tech Usage

1. **Reduces Digital Dependency** —Mindfulness about technology use helps prevent compulsive behaviors, such as checking social media out of habit rather than necessity.

2. **Enhances Presence in Relationships** – Mindful tech habits ensure that conversations and connections remain meaningful and uninterrupted.

3. **Encourages Conscious Consumption** – Rather than passively engaging with technology, mindful users select content and platforms that enrich their lives.

4. **Improves Mental Well-Being** – Using technology intentionally reduces stress, anxiety, and feeling overwhelmed.

Strategies for Mindful Tech Usage

1. **Establish "Tech Breaks" Throughout the Day** —Designate specific times for checking emails, browsing social media, and responding to messages instead of constantly doing so.

2. **Use Technology with a Purpose** – Before picking up your phone or opening a new tab, ask yourself, "What am I using this for?" If there's no clear purpose, consider putting the device away.

3. **Limit Multitasking** – Focus on one digital task at a time to enhance productivity and reduce cognitive overload.

4. **Engage in Digital Detoxes** —Set aside periods (e.g., a weekend or a day per week) to go completely offline.

5. **Make Mealtime Screen-Free** – Focus on eating and engaging

with those around you instead of checking devices.

6. **Practice Single-Tasking** – Instead of switching between multiple apps and tasks, focus on completing one thing at a time to improve efficiency and presence.

7. **Use Reminders for Mindfulness** – Set notifications that remind you to take deep breaths, stretch, or check in with your emotional state before continuing digital engagement.

Mindful tech usage fosters a balanced relationship with digital tools, ensuring they enhance life rather than distract from it.

Final Thoughts: Taking Charge of Your Digital Experience

In the digital era, technology can either be a tool for enrichment or a source of overwhelm. By setting screen time limits, curating a positive digital space, and practicing mindful tech usage, individuals can reclaim control over their digital experiences and improve their overall well-being.

Thriving in a digital world is not about eliminating technology but about using it with awareness and intention. When individuals cultivate a mindful approach to technology, they unlock the ability to stay connected without feeling consumed, leading to a healthier, more fulfilling life.

Section 3: Using Technology to Thrive

Technology is often viewed as a double-edged sword. While excessive use can lead to distractions and mental fatigue, mindful engagement with digital tools can significantly enhance well-being, productivity, and personal growth. By leveraging mental health apps, building digital boundaries, and staying intentional online, individuals can cultivate a more balanced relationship with technology that supports their overall well-being.

Mental Health Apps and Tools: Leveraging Technology for Well-Being

The rise of digital wellness tools has made mental health support more accessible than ever. From meditation apps to mood trackers, technology can provide valuable assistance in managing stress, improving focus, and fostering emotional resilience.

Benefits of Mental Health Apps

1. **Accessibility** – Provides on-demand support anytime, anywhere.
2. **Personalized Insights** – Uses data tracking to identify patterns in mood and behavior.
3. **Guided Support** – Offers structured mindfulness, therapy, and emotional regulation programs.
4. **Affordability** – Many apps provide free or low-cost mental health resources.
5. **Anonymity** – Allows users to explore mental health solutions privately.

Popular Mental Health Apps and Tools

1. **Meditation and Mindfulness:**
    - *Headspace* – Guided meditation and mindfulness techniques.
    - *Calm* – Sleep stories, breathing exercises, and relaxation techniques.

2. **Mood and Habit Tracking:**
    - *Moodfit* – Personalized tools to track mood patterns and improve emotional well-being.
    - *Daylio* – A mood and habit tracker that promotes self-awareness.

3. **Cognitive Behavioral Therapy (CBT) Apps:**
    - *Woebot* – AI-powered chatbot offering evidence-based emotional support.
    - *Sanvello* – Self-guided CBT techniques for anxiety and stress management.
4. **Focus and Productivity:**
    - *Forest* – Encourages focused work sessions by planting virtual trees that grow when distractions are avoided.
    - *Freedom* – Blocks distracting websites and apps to enhance concentration.

By integrating these digital tools into daily routines, individuals can cultivate mindfulness, emotional regulation, and overall mental well-being.

Building Digital Boundaries: Creating Tech-Free Zones

While technology is essential today, excessive screen time can disrupt mental clarity, reduce productivity, and affect relationships. Establishing digital boundaries helps individuals regain control over their tech habits and fosters a healthier balance between online and offline life.

Why Digital Boundaries Matter

1. **Improves Focus and Productivity** – Minimizes distractions and enhances deep work.
2. **Supports Mental Health** – Reduces digital fatigue and stress caused by constant connectivity.
3. **Enhances Sleep Quality** – Less screen time before bed promotes better sleep patterns.
4. **Strengthens Relationships** – Encourages deeper in-person interactions by minimizing device distractions.

Practical Steps to Establish Tech-Free Zones

1. **Define No-Screen Areas:**
   - Designate specific spaces in the home, such as bedrooms or dining areas, as tech-free zones.
   - Establish a "device-free dinner" rule to encourage meaningful conversation.

2. **Implement Time-Based Restrictions:**
   - Set boundaries around when digital devices can be used (e.g., no screens an hour before bedtime).
   - Utilize features like Apple's Screen Time or Android's Digital Wellbeing to monitor and limit usage.

3. **Use Physical Reminders:**
   - Place a basket or charging station outside the bedrooms to store phones overnight.
   - Use an analog alarm clock instead of relying on a smartphone.

4. **Schedule Regular Digital Detoxes:**
   - Dedicate one day per week to unplugging from social media and unnecessary screen exposure.
   - Engage in offline hobbies such as reading, hiking, or journaling to reconnect with the present moment.

5. **Set App and Notification Limits:**
   - Turn off non-essential notifications to minimize constant digital interruptions.
   - Uninstall apps that contribute to mindless scrolling or digital clutter.

Establishing digital boundaries creates intentional breaks from screen time, allowing individuals to reset mentally, connect with others, and focus on what truly matters.

Staying Intentional Online: Using Technology to Enhance, Not Distract

Technology should serve as a tool for growth and connection rather than a source of distraction. By adopting mindful digital habits, individuals can use technology to enhance productivity, creativity, and well-being.

The Importance of Intentional Tech Use

1. **Prevents Mindless Scrolling** – Reduces wasted time spent on unproductive online activities.

2. **Encourages Meaningful Engagement** – Focuses on quality interactions rather than passive consumption.

3. **Boosts Mental Well-Being** – Prioritizes uplifting and informative content over negativity.

4. **Enhances Learning and Creativity** – Leverages technology for self-improvement and skill-building.

Strategies for Staying Intentional Online

1. **Set Clear Objectives for Online Use:**
   - Ask yourself, "Why am I using this app or platform?" before engaging.
   - To avoid aimless scrolling, define digital goals like networking, learning, or relaxation.

2. **Curate Your Digital Experience:**
   - Follow accounts that inspire and educate rather than provoke stress or comparison.
   - Unsubscribe from email lists and social media pages that don't add value.

3. **Engage with Purpose:**
   - Prioritize active participation (commenting, creating,

and discussing) over passive consumption (endless scrolling and binge-watching).
- Use social media to foster meaningful connections rather than just absorbing content.

4. **Practice Digital Minimalism:**
    - Remove unnecessary apps that don't serve a meaningful purpose.
    - Set times to check emails and social media rather than constantly being connected.

5. **Balance Online and Offline Activities:**
    - Integrate real-world experiences, such as exercise, hobbies, and in-person interactions, to complement digital engagement.
    - Avoid replacing face-to-face interactions with digital communication whenever possible.

Individuals can use technology to ensure that digital tools enrich rather than detract from their daily lives.

Final Thoughts: Leveraging Technology for a Healthier Life

When used with mindfulness and intentionality, technology can enhance well-being, creativity, and productivity. By leveraging mental health apps, setting digital boundaries, and adopting purposeful online habits, individuals can create a tech experience that supports their goals and enriches their lives.

Thriving in a digital world requires a conscious approach to technology. Instead of allowing screens to dictate daily habits, individuals can make intentional choices that empower them to live more fulfilling and balanced lives. By harnessing the benefits of technology while minimizing its drawbacks, anyone can use digital tools as a force for personal growth and well-being.

Chapter 8: The Mental Fitness Blueprint for Life

"What you get by achieving your goals is not as important as what you become by achieving your goals." – Zig Ziglar

Section 1: Maintaining Momentum

Achieving mental fitness is not a one-time event but an ongoing process. The journey does not end when new habits are formed; it requires continuous effort to maintain momentum. This section reviews key takeaways, leveraging small successes to create lasting change and embracing consistency over perfection as the foundation of sustainable mental well-being.

Reviewing What You've Learned: Key Takeaways from the Book

Throughout this book, we have explored the essential components of mental fitness. Individuals can cultivate resilience, clarity, and purpose by integrating these principles into daily life. Here are some of the most significant lessons:

1. The Mind-Body Connection

- Physical health directly influences mental wellness. Sleep, nutrition, and movement are critical components of a balanced mind.
- Stress hormones like cortisol can be managed through relaxation techniques, mindfulness, and rest.

2. Emotional Regulation and Awareness

- Recognizing emotional triggers helps respond thoughtfully rather than impulsively.
- Practicing gratitude and optimism reshapes brain pathways, fostering resilience and positive thinking.
- Letting go of negative patterns, including self-doubt and past grievances, creates space for growth.

3. Strengthening Relationships and Social Connection

- Meaningful relationships are crucial for emotional support and mental stability.
- Setting boundaries and recognizing toxic patterns protect emotional well-being.
- Active listening and clear communication enhance connection and understanding.

4. Digital Well-Being and Intentionality

- Technology can enhance or hinder mental fitness depending on how it is used.

- Setting digital boundaries, curating a positive online space, and practicing mindful tech usage help maintain balance.

5. The Power of Purpose and Intention

- Aligning daily actions with personal values fosters fulfillment and long-term satisfaction.
- Overcoming distractions and prioritizing what matters most strengthens one's sense of purpose.
- Resilience is built through overcoming challenges and learning from setbacks.

By reflecting on these lessons, individuals can reinforce their commitment to mental fitness and identify areas that require further growth.

Building on Success: How Small Wins Create Lasting Change

The path to mental fitness is not about grand, sweeping transformations. Instead, minor, incremental improvements lead to significant and lasting change. Recognizing and celebrating these small wins builds confidence and motivation.

Why Small Wins Matter

- **Reinforces Positive Behavior** – Every small success strengthens the neural pathways associated with productive habits.
- **Creates Momentum** – Success, no matter how minor, fuels motivation to keep going.
- **Reduces Overwhelm** – Breaking big goals into smaller, achievable tasks makes them more manageable.

How to Leverage Small Wins

- **Set Micro-Goals** – Instead of focusing on a major

achievement, break it down into smaller steps. For example:

- Rather than aiming to "reduce stress," start by practicing deep breathing for two minutes daily.
- Instead of attempting to "become more social," commit to one meaningful weekly conversation.

- **Track Progress** – Keeping a journal or using habit-tracking apps can reinforce consistency and highlight growth.
- **Builds Confidence** – Recognizing progress fosters a sense of accomplishment and self-efficacy.

Consistency Over Perfection: The Importance of Showing Up Daily

A common roadblock in personal development is the pursuit of perfection. The belief that every action must be flawless often leads to procrastination, frustration, and, ultimately, giving up. Mental fitness thrives on consistency, not perfection.

The Pitfalls of Perfectionism

1. **Leads to Burnout** – Setting unrealistic standards creates stress and exhaustion.
2. **Causes Paralysis** – Fear of failure can prevent individuals from taking action altogether.
3. **Fuels Self-Doubt** – Constantly falling short of perfection can lead to negative self-talk and decreased motivation.
   - **Celebrate Every Step** – Acknowledge and reward progress, whether completing a task, sticking to a habit, or handling a challenge well.
   - **Discourages Experimentation** – A rigid mindset limits growth and prevents learning from mistakes.

By continuously recognizing progress, individuals remain engaged in their mental fitness journey and sustain motivation.

Why Consistency is More Important

1. **Builds Habits Gradually** – Small, regular efforts become ingrained habits that require less effort over time.

2. **Encourages Adaptability** – Imperfect action allows for flexibility and learning from experiences.

3. **Reduces Pressure** – Accepting progress over perfection removes the stress of always needing to get things right.

4. **Strengthens Commitment** – Showing up daily, even when motivation is low, reinforces discipline and long-term success.

How to Cultivate Consistency

1. **Lower the Bar for Success** —If motivation is lacking, try adopting the most miniature version of a habit rather than skipping it entirely (e.g., meditating for one minute instead of ten).

2. **Use Habit Stacking** – Attach new habits to existing ones (e.g., practicing gratitude right after brushing teeth).

3. **Adopt a Growth Mindset** – Embrace mistakes as learning opportunities rather than failures.

4. **Develop a Routine** – Establishing structured habits minimizes decision fatigue and makes healthy choices automatic.

5. **Accept Imperfection** – Progress is rarely linear. Some days will be more challenging than others, and that's okay.

Individuals can build sustainable mental fitness habits that withstand ups and downs by prioritizing consistency over perfection.

Final Thoughts: A Lifelong Commitment to Mental Fitness

Mental fitness is not a destination but a continuous journey. Individuals can create lasting, positive change in their lives by reviewing what they have learned, celebrating small wins, and maintaining consistency.

- **Reflect Regularly** – Take time to assess progress and adjust strategies as needed.

- **Stay Committed** – Mental fitness requires ongoing effort and intentionality.

- **Seek Support When Needed** – Connecting with supportive individuals and seeking professional guidance can enhance growth.

Ultimately, maintaining momentum comes down to showing up every day with intention. Some days will be easier than others, but every step taken contributes to long-term mental resilience and well-being.

By embracing these principles, individuals can cultivate a fulfilling, mentally fit life that thrives on growth, connection, and purpose.

Section 2: Sustaining Mental Fitness Long-Term

Mental fitness is not a destination but a lifelong journey. As life evolves, challenges arise, priorities shift, and new opportunities present themselves. Mental fitness over the long term requires adaptability, self-awareness, and a strong connection to personal purpose. This section explores how to stay mentally resilient through life's changes, perform regular mental health check-ins, and ensure that one's "why" remains a guiding force in decision-making and daily actions.

Adapting to Life's Changes: Staying Flexible Through Transitions

Change is a constant in life. Career shifts, relationship changes, aging, personal growth, and unexpected life events require mental agility. While change can be unsettling, developing flexibility in thought and behavior can help individuals maintain mental well-being during transitions.

Why Adaptability is Key to Mental Fitness

1. **Reduces Stress** – Resistance to change can create anxiety, whereas embracing change fosters resilience.

2. **Encourages Growth** – Change presents opportunities for learning and self-improvement.

3. **Enhances Problem-Solving** – Flexible thinking leads to creative solutions for new challenges.

4. **Strengthens Emotional Resilience** – Adaptable individuals recover more quickly from setbacks.

Strategies for Staying Mentally Flexible

1. **Shift Your Perspective** – Instead of viewing change as a disruption, reframe it as an opportunity for growth.

2. **Develop Coping Strategies** – Build a toolkit of stress-reduction techniques such as mindfulness, deep breathing, and physical movement.

3. **Maintain a Learning Mindset** – Embrace curiosity and view challenges as opportunities to develop new skills.

4. **Stay Connected** – Seeking support from friends, family, or professional networks can ease transitions.

5. **Let Go of Perfectionism** – Accepting that not everything will go as planned reduces frustration and builds emotional resilience.

6. **Create a New Routine** – Establishing structure during periods of change can provide a sense of stability and control.

Adapting to change with an open mind and a flexible attitude enables individuals to navigate life's uncertainties while maintaining mental clarity and stability.

Checking in with Yourself: Regular Mental Health Audits

Just as physical health requires regular check-ups, mental health benefits from periodic self-assessments, regular mental health audits help individuals identify stressors, recognize areas for improvement, and reinforce healthy habits.

Why Mental Health Audits Matter

1. **Promotes Self-Awareness** – Understanding emotional and mental states allows for proactive adjustments.
2. **Prevents Burnout** – Regular check-ins can catch early warning signs of stress and exhaustion.
3. **Encourages Balance** – Helps maintain equilibrium between work, relationships, and personal well-being.
4. **Supports Goal Alignment** – Ensures daily actions align with long-term values and aspirations.

How to Conduct a Mental Health Audit

1. **Assess Your Emotional State**
    - How am I feeling emotionally today?
    - Have I been experiencing prolonged stress, sadness, or anxiety?

2. **Evaluate Stress Levels**
    - What are my current stressors?
    - How effectively am I managing stress?
    - Do I need to implement more self-care practices?

3. **Review Energy and Physical Well-Being**
    - Am I getting enough rest, nutrition, and physical activity?
    - Do I feel energized or constantly fatigued?

4. **Analyze Relationships and Social Support**
    - Am I engaging in meaningful connections with family and friends?
    - Are there any relationships that are draining or toxic?
    - Do I need to seek support from others?

5. **Reflect on Work and Purpose**
    - Am I satisfied with my career or personal projects?
    - Is my work-life balance healthy?
    - Do I feel a sense of fulfillment in what I do daily?

6. **Identify Necessary Adjustments**
    - What changes can I make to improve my mental well-being?
    - Which habits should I continue, and which should I modify?
    - What boundaries do I need to set to protect my mental fitness?

Setting a Routine for Mental Health Check-Ins

- **Daily** – Quick emotional check-ins (e.g., How am I feeling right now?)
- **Weekly** – Reflect on energy levels, stressors, and self-care habits.
- **Monthly** – Assess larger patterns, evaluate goals, and make necessary adjustments.
- **Annually** – A profound reflection on life direction, personal growth, and long-term mental fitness strategies.

By regularly practicing mental health audits, individuals can maintain greater control over their emotional well-being and make necessary adjustments to sustain mental fitness long-term.

Revisiting Your Purpose: Keeping Your "Why" Front and Center

Purpose is a powerful motivator that provides direction and meaning in life. However, as circumstances change, it is essential to revisit and refine one's purpose to ensure it remains aligned with personal values and aspirations.

Why Revisiting Purpose Matters

1. **Keeps Motivation Strong** – A clear sense of purpose prevents stagnation and provides inspiration.
2. **Enhances Decision-Making** – When priorities are clear, making choices that align with one's values becomes more manageable.
3. **Encourages Resilience** – Purpose-driven individuals can navigate adversity with a stronger sense of direction.
4. **Fosters Greater Fulfillment** – Aligning actions with core values leads to a more profound satisfaction in life.

How to Reconnect with Your Purpose

1. **Reflect on Meaningful Moments**
   - When have I felt the most fulfilled in my life?
   - What activities or experiences bring me deep satisfaction?
2. **Identify Core Values**
   - What principles guide my decisions?
   - Have my values changed over time?
3. **Assess Current Alignment**
   - Am I living in a way that aligns with my purpose?
   - Are there areas of my life where I feel disconnected

from what matters most?

4. **Set Purposeful Goals**
    - What small actions can I take daily to align with my purpose?
    - How can I incorporate my values into my work, relationships, and personal growth?

5. **Adapt and Refine as Needed**
    - Purpose is not static; it evolves with experience and growth.
    - Regularly revisiting and adjusting the purpose ensures it remains relevant.

Keeping purpose front and center, individuals maintain a sense of direction and fulfillment, even amid life's uncertainties.

Final Thoughts: A Lifelong Commitment to Mental Fitness

Sustaining mental fitness long-term requires intentionality, self-awareness, and adaptability. By embracing change, regularly checking in on mental health, and staying connected to personal purpose, individuals can build a resilient mindset that supports lifelong well-being.

- **Stay Flexible** – Life will continue to change, and adapting to those changes is key to staying mentally strong.
- **Check In Regularly** – Self-assessments help maintain balance and prevent burnout.
- **Keep Your Purpose Clear** – Revisiting "why" ensures ongoing motivation and fulfillment.

Mental fitness is a lifelong practice that evolves with experience, challenges, and personal growth. By making intentional adjustments and remaining committed to mental well-being, individuals can lead lives that are not only resilient but deeply fulfilling.

Section 3: Thriving Beyond the Noise

In today's fast-paced world, external pressures, distractions, and the constant demands of modern life can easily overwhelm one. Thriving beyond the noise means cultivating a life of balance, purpose, and meaning. It involves integrating everything learned throughout this journey, inspiring others through personal growth, and embracing the process rather than solely focusing on the end goal. This section explores how to live a balanced, purposeful life, serve as a mental health role model, and celebrate the journey toward mental fitness.

Living a Balanced, Purposeful Life: Putting It All Together

Balance and purpose are the foundations of a fulfilling life. While achieving mental fitness requires intentionality, it does not mean rigidly adhering to a single formula. Instead, it involves continuously adjusting to life's evolving circumstances while staying connected to one's core values.

What Does Balance Look Like?

A balanced life is not about perfection—it's about harmony. It means ensuring that different aspects of life, such as career, relationships, health, and personal growth, complement each other rather than compete.

1. **Emotional Well-Being** – Managing stress, practicing self-care, and allowing space for relaxation.
2. **Physical Health** – Prioritizing sleep, nutrition, and movement to sustain energy and vitality.
3. **Meaningful Relationships** – Investing in healthy, supportive connections that uplift and nurture personal growth.
4. **Personal Development** – Continuously learning, evolving,

and striving toward new goals.

5. **Purpose and Fulfillment** – Engaging in activities that align with core values and contribute to something larger than oneself.

Practical Steps to Achieve Balance

1. **Define Priorities** – Identify what matters most and allocate time and energy accordingly.

2. **Set Boundaries** – Protect mental and emotional space by saying no to unnecessary stressors.

3. **Practice Mindfulness** – Engage in the present moment rather than being consumed by past regrets or future worries.

4. **Establish Routines** – Create daily habits that support well-being and provide structure.

5. **Embrace Flexibility** – Adapt to life's changes with resilience and openness.

Living a balanced and purposeful life is about integration—combining the tools, habits, and insights gained from the mental fitness journey and applying them consistently to create lasting fulfillment.

Inspiring Others Through Your Growth: Being a Mental Health Role Model

One of the most potent aspects of personal growth is its ability to inspire and uplift others. By embodying mental fitness principles, individuals can become role models for their families, friends, and communities, fostering a culture of well-being and resilience.

Why Leading by Example Matters

1. **Breaks the Stigma Around Mental Health** – Openly discussing mental well-being encourages others to seek help and practice self-care.

2. **Creates a Ripple Effect** – Positive behaviors and attitudes influence those around us, leading to healthier communities.

3. **Encourages Vulnerability and Authenticity** – Sharing personal struggles and triumphs fosters deeper connections and mutual support.

4. **Empower Others to Take Action** – Witnessing someone prioritize mental fitness motivates others to do the same.

Ways to Inspire Others

1. **Share Your Story** —Discussing mental fitness openly can encourage others, whether through conversation, writing, or social media.

2. **Be a Supportive Presence** – Listen, validate, and encourage those struggling.

3. **Model Healthy Habits** – Demonstrate self-care, emotional regulation, and mindfulness in everyday life.

4. **Encourage Growth** – Recommend books, podcasts, or resources that have been helpful in your journey.

5. **Practice Compassion** – Approach others with understanding and patience, knowing everyone's journey is different.

By embodying the principles of mental fitness, individuals enhance their well-being and uplift those around them, creating a collective movement toward healthier, more resilient communities.

Celebrating the Journey: Embracing the Process, Not Just the Result

Too often, people become fixated on reaching a specific goal, whether reducing stress, improving relationships, or finding purpose. While goals are important, true fulfillment comes from embracing the journey itself. Mental fitness is a lifelong practice, not a destination.

The Importance of Enjoying the Process

1. **Prevents Burnout** – Focusing solely on outcomes can lead to frustration and exhaustion.

2. **Enhances Gratitude** – Recognizing progress fosters an appreciation for small victories.

3. **Builds Resilience** – Learning from setbacks strengthens perseverance and adaptability.

4. **Encourages Continuous Growth** – Embracing the journey keeps curiosity and learning alive.

How to Celebrate the Journey

1. **Acknowledge Progress** —Take time to reflect on how far you've come, even if there is room for improvement.

2. **Find Joy in Daily Practices** – Appreciate the benefits of small habits, such as journaling, meditation, or mindful movement.

3. **Shift Perspective on Challenges** – View obstacles as learning opportunities rather than failures.

4. **Celebrate Small Wins** – Recognize achievements, no matter how minor, and use them as motivation to continue.

5. **Be Kind to Yourself** – Allow for imperfection and self-compassion throughout the journey.

Thriving beyond the noise means shifting focus from external pressures and unrealistic expectations to internal fulfillment and personal growth. It's about creating a meaningful, balanced, and prosperous life with purpose—one step at a time.

Final Thoughts: Embracing a Life of Mental Fitness

Mental fitness is a continuous, evolving process that requires commitment, adaptability, and self-awareness. Individuals can create a fulfilling and resilient life by integrating balance, inspiring others, and celebrating the journey.

- **Live with Intention** – Align daily actions with values and purpose.
- **Be a Beacon of Positivity** – Inspire others by leading with authenticity and openness.
- **Enjoy the Ride** – Recognize that actual growth happens in the process, not just the destination.

By thriving beyond the noise, individuals can cultivate a mentally strong and deeply rewarding life, inspiring those around them to do the same.

www.ingramcontent.com/pod-product-compliance
Lightning Source LLC
Chambersburg PA
CBHW070547090426
42735CB00013B/3096